PULL OF THE THREAD
TEXTILE TRAVELS
OF A GENERATION

PULL OF THE THREAD
TEXTILE TRAVELS
OF A GENERATION

Sheila Fruman

Hali

Pull of the Thread:
Textile Travels of a Generation

Published and produced by Hali Publications Ltd.,
6 Sylvester Path, London E8 1EN, United Kingdom

Designed by Anikst Design, London

British Library Cataloguing-in-Publication Data:
a catalogue record for this book is available from the
British Library

ISBN 9781898113874

Cover: ikat robes from Uzbekistan from the collection of Pip Rau.
Suzani detail on the frontispiece: Cleveland Museum of Art,
2016.89, Gift of John and Fausta Eskenazi in honor of Louise W.
Mackie and in celebration of the museum's centennial.
Embroidery detail opposite Preface: Steven Cohen collection.

*The texts in this book are based on interviews carried out by the
author in 2019*

*The opinions expressed in this publication are those of the author
and interviewees and do not necessarily reflect the views or
positions of any entities they represent or Hali Publications Ltd.*

Contents

FOR ROSEANNA AND RUBY

Acknowledgements

I am indebted to the dealers and collectors featured here who were so generous with their time and allowed me to write their stories. I also appreciate their efforts to dig through dusty boxes and reach out to long-lost travel companions to find photos from a time when not many people were taking them.

My thanks to those featured in the 'interiors' chapter, whose inspired use of materials that had once seemed exotic demonstrates how such textiles can reach far beyond their origins to connect different people in disparate places.

Most of all, I want to acknowledge the many unnamed women and men who made, shared and traded their family heirlooms and handmade treasures. Their generosity and openness to strangers contributed to an enriching cultural exchange and an enduring legacy of increased knowledge, appreciation and understanding.

When I proposed the book to Ben Evans at Hali Publications, he was not only willing to take a risk on an unusual subject but had interesting ideas for how to provide context and continuity to the individual stories. That's how Mary Schoeser, for whose expertise and contribution I am grateful, came to write the final chapter. Malin Lonnberg smoothed out the rough edges in my writing, sourced photos, and was the liaison between me and Misha An kst, the designer. Malin was exceptionally capable, resourceful, and most pleasant to work with. My thanks to Misha for so beautifully presenting the material.

When the National Democratic Institute first sent me to work in Algeria almost a quarter of a century ago, it opened my eyes to a whole new world of possibilities that, ultimately, led to me write this book. Thank you, Ken Wollack and other NDI colleagues, for your confidence in me over the years as I worked in many different countries.

Susan Scollay was enthusiastic from the time she first read my proposal for the book. Her keen interest helped me keep going from start to finish. Many friends and family encouraged me to resume the project after a year-long hiatus during the pandemic, and I am grateful to all of them for that support.

The legacy of the dealers featured here, as well as that of many others, is extensive – rug clubs, conferences, programmes, classes, tours and scholarship – and I was a beneficiary. The Hajji Baba Club of New York provided ongoing camaraderie with a wonderfully quirky community of experts and like-minded enthusiasts. Other rug clubs, institutions and organisations, like the Textile Museum Associates of Southern California, the New England Rug Society, the Oxford Asian Textile Group, the George Washington Textile Museum, the Textile Research Centre, the International Conference on Oriental Carpets, the Textile Museum of Canada and the Victoria and Albert Museum increased my appreciation and knowledge and kept me inspired.

HALI magazine is an outstanding innovation from the period, which has grown to include the publication of numerous books and the organisation of fairs and tours that bring together a global community of antique carpet and textile dealers, collectors, curators and enthusiasts. They have been an important and supportive touchstone for me in the world of oriental carpets and textiles.

My Fridays at TAMAM, when the owners handed me the keys to the shop, was a weekly reminder that seeing and touching antique, handmade indigenous materials lifts the spirit and soothes the soul. I am grateful to Elizabeth Hewitt, Clare Louise Frost and Hüseyin Kaplan for trusting me with their treasures.

Kim Roberts provided a safe haven in his beautiful home, when I desperately needed such a space in order to finalise the project.

No words are enough to thank my daughter, Roseanna Roberts, for always being an insightful critic and my biggest cheerleader.

Sheila Fruman

Preface

A meandering journey across Asia in a brightly painted car was almost a rite of passage for the tune in, drop out youth of the late sixties and seventies. This was the Silk Road's hippie wave. They followed the trail of storied Western travellers such as Robert Byron, Nicolas Bouvier and Josephine Powell, who had written about, or photographed, places whose light and landscape so dazzled their vision that they saw the world anew. This appeal was not lost on the sixties generation. Colourful, rebellious, open-hearted, these flower children were unique in their counter-cultural stance and their affinity for the nomadic tribes at the edges of empires. They tended to aim for Afghanistan, a country that had been closed off to Europe until the 1920s. Kabul was both the ends of the earth and the centre of the world – the hub of fabric trade with spokes into Pakistan, Central Asia, India and Iran. The political events in this region, from the ongoing fallout of the partition of India to the Iranian Revolution and the Soviet invasion of Afghanistan, brought an ever-changing mix of textiles into the bazaars. In the following decades the Soviet Union would loosen its grip on Central Asia and more merchandise would appear on the market.

A hippie herself, Sheila Fruman convincingly links the current popularity of kilims, suzanis and ikats in both fashion and home décor to the handful of intrepid textile dealers portrayed in this volume. Their stories are as varied as the weaves, prints and embroideries they brought to the European and American sensibility. Driven by the lure of adventure, commercial opportunities or simply self-discovery, these kindred free spirits had an eye for unappreciated crafts, the perseverance to develop deep expertise, and the calling to share their passion with a wide audience. Some, like Pip Rau, Steven Cohen, Kate Fitz Gibbon and Andy Hale, were, like Fruman, explorers of Afghanistan. Joss Graham and Frank Ames focused on India. Others wandered about the region according to happenstance – the nomads of the trade. Whether they began on a whim or an academic impulse, these are all stories of learning, anchored in an appreciation for indigenous craft and informed by decades of life on the road. Behind every one of the dealers in this book there was a network of local textile experts and trusted 'pickers' who would comb the countryside for treasures. To assemble such a team was a skill given to very few and based on an ethnographic understanding that was self-taught.

What is perhaps the most striking feature of this series of portraits is how they converge to reveal an idiosyncratic generation of dealers turned collectors. All made important and even essential contributions to their fields, publishing books, staging exhibitions, and often gifting items to major institutions such as the V&A and Met. Ikats became prized museum items, but other tribal artforms were similarly elevated to scholarly status and broadly appreciated. Western interest led in turn to a revival of local handicraft and the preservation of traditional weaving techniques particularly in Uzbekistan. The Day-Glo Land Rovers may be long gone, but Fruman's book lets us rattle down that road again and remember that every generation seems to turn up new interests and adds to the never-ending cycle of global exchange along the Silk Road.

Nathalie Farman-Farma

Introduction

'Travelling outgrows its motives. It soon proves sufficient in itself. You think you are making a trip, but soon it is making you – or unmaking you.'
Nicolas Bouvier, 'The Way of the World'

How did a 19th-century suzani from Uzbekistan, a country on the other side of the world, end up in my 21st-century apartment in Brooklyn? This book is the answer.

I didn't know it then, but the seeds for my love of suzanis, and the other carpet and textile types shown here, were planted in 1969 when I travelled overland from London to India. It would be many years later before I grasped their meaning as a material connection to my own and our shared history, a subversive means of resistance to persecution, a balm of beauty for suffering, and a generational vehicle of cultural meaning.

In 1969 I was a naïve twenty-year-old hippie, fresh out of university with a BA in Sociology from the University of British Columbia. I had wanted to go to Afghanistan since Grade 10, although I didn't know why, or even where it was. It made no sense considering I'm a nice Jewish girl from a middle-class family who grew up in Regina, Saskatchewan, the middle of nowhere on the Canadian prairies. My parents emigrated from Russia in the 1920s when they were very young and that was the last time anyone in the family travelled anywhere. Travelling was done to escape, not to explore.

I had no idea what I wanted to do with the rest of my life except travel. I was following a deep inner voice that was plugged into the era's zeitgeist of whimsical adventure and unbridled curiosity.

Turn on, tune in, drop out, was a rallying cry for much of the post-Second World War generation that grew up in a period of economic prosperity. It coincided with open borders and a global political trend that welcomed travel by Westerners to Middle Eastern and Asian countries. By the 1960s, the stars had lined up to inspire a modern-day pilgrimage from Turkey to India, never before so readily available, to a generation of young people intent on seeking adventure.

In the late 1970s, travel became more difficult and dangerous once Russia occupied Afghanistan, the Ayatollah Khomeini was ensconced in Iran, and anti-Western extremism gradually took hold in Pakistan; but, for a brief period, travel was the way forward for a significant number of young Westerners.

The world was there to be explored and we were anxious to do it. Boeing jets doubled speed and halved fares across the Atlantic. Marshall McLuhan talked about a 'global village'. Betty Friedan and Gloria Steinem called for 'women's liberation'. The Beatles flew to India. Bob Dylan sang 'The times they are a-changin'…' Borders almost everywhere were wide open to young people with a few dollars or quid in their pocket – often provided by a grant from the government[1] – whether you were searching for nirvana or just an unconventional escape from 'the shackles of tradition'.[2]

I worked at the university's psychiatric hospital over the summer to earn money before setting off, in September, for the other side of the world. I had no map, no plan and no idea how to get there, since there was, as yet, no Trip Advisor, Google Map, or even Lonely Planet.

My high-school friend Julie, who had a no-strings-attached Canada Council grant for artists, joined me. We hitch hiked our way from Amsterdam, through the former Socialist Federal Republic of Yugoslavia, to Athens where I had lined up a job teaching English. After the first day, I threw in the towel and we took off for the island of Crete. A big house we rented in Heraklion, the capital, soon became a gathering place for other wayward travellers. They told us about living in some caves in Matala, which sounded like a good time, and we decided to see for ourselves. We had just missed Joni Mitchell, another Saskatchewan expat, whose song 'Carey' later immortalised the place.

opposite
Sheila Fruman

By December we had finally decided to go to Afghanistan. We arrived by train in Istanbul, enticed by the kilims, carpets and textiles to be found there; but my main preoccupation was finding a way to get to Afghanistan. One night at the Pudding Shop in Sultanahmet – a notorious hang-out for Western hippies impetuously schlepping across unsuspecting foreign lands seeking the exotic unknown – we met two American guys. They were driving through Turkey, Iran and Afghanistan to Pakistan with the nefarious purpose of loading up their vehicle with hashish and shipping it back to the US via Karachi on the Arabian Sea. I blithely ignored the obvious risks of smuggling drugs and we climbed on board for the ride.

The men were on a mission and not much interested in sightseeing or shopping for the world-renowned carpets of Iran. We whizzed through the country, arriving in Afghanistan where my youthful curiosity was overtaken by the men's determination to procure hashish and leave as quickly as possible.

It was bitterly cold in Kabul and I stared, with disbelief, at scantily clad men on the street selling little books of matches and individual pieces of string, as we returned from a Christmas Day turkey dinner at the Intercontinental Hotel, the best dining room in the city, to our freezing hotel room. Kabul, then, had a reputation for being liberal, where young women could go out alone, dress as they wished and attend university, but that was a very different picture from the poverty and suffering I saw there that winter.

We drove through the Khyber Pass from Afghanistan into the North West Frontier Province of Pakistan,[3] arriving at the town of Mingora in the district of Swat. A former princely state, Swat is famous for its natural beauty and exceptional embroidered textiles. The men were toting Kalashnikovs slung casually over their shoulders, and wearing striped black-and-white scarves wrapped turban-style around their heads. Their loose-fitting shirts hung over baggy pyjama-like bottoms, known as shalwar kameez. They had moustaches or big, bushy beards which had turned brilliant orange from being dyed with henna.

We also presented a dramatic image. The Land Rover was painted with psychedelic suns and towering flames in bright, Day-Glo hues. We were an itinerant caravan of blaring sound and blinding colour swerving our way along the perilous mud roads and through the swirling dust in the shadow of the Hindu Kush mountains. The men looked intimidating to me, but it's hard to imagine how we looked to them in our eccentric garb and with our freewheeling ways.

My long dark hair was a tangle of curls cascading over a turquoise silk-lined spotted lynx fur coat I had picked up at a market in Kabul.

Ornate Afghan silver jewellery dangled from my ears and covered my hands. My blue eyes were ringed with the black kohl commonly worn by both men and women in the region. Under the coat I wore a vintage white silk Afghan dress with hand-embroidered magenta and black bib and stitched trim around the cuffs and hem.

Julie shimmered in a stunning white wool shoulder cape covered in sparkling shisha mirrors and fine embroidery picked up in Iran that she wore over a bejewelled, plush-green velvet top. Her blonde hair, after I applied henna, complemented the men's flaming orange beards.

We met in a teahouse with seven or eight burly, armed, ethnic Pashtuns. They were swathed in beautiful pure-wool blankets thrown over their shalwar kameez in subdued neutral shades of camel, taupe and bone, to fend off the bitter cold. Instead of a turban some wore the traditional Afghan pakol – a soft, flat-topped woollen hat – in earthy hues of brown, black, grey, ivory and a unique red obtained from walnut dye.

The tribal areas were reputed to be dangerous, and Pashtuns known to be fierce fighters, but the 'Khan', one of the men at the teahouse, graciously invited us to be guests in his home in keeping with the time-honoured Pashtun custom of hospitality to visitors. The men treated Julie and me as though we were a third sex – female but with male privileges – an arrangement that was the best of both worlds in this highly stratified society where women and men each had clearly defined different roles.

We were seated in a circle on the ground on a sufra – a special cloth for meals – eating with our hands and tackling big pieces of naan bread, though we were not nearly as adroit as our hosts. Dining tables and chairs were foreign in this part of Pakistan, as was cutlery.

During the meal, I admired a magnificent rich-brown, pure camel-wool coat worn by a rather tall, dark and handsome guest. No sooner did I utter the compliment than he removed it and presented it to me as a gift. Despite my protests, he refused to take it back, and I became the owner of a large, luxurious garment suitable for someone twice my size. I was thereafter careful to watch what I said, fearing my admiration would lead to more such acts of generosity from these exceptionally hospitable hosts.

By now I was becoming aware of my attraction to the magnificent range of textiles I had seen along the way and among the people of the Swat Valley – embroidered silk dresses, mirrored shawls, the finest woven wool hats and coats – but I did not imagine them in my future. I was searching for something which didn't yet include textiles.

At sunset we set off with the men in horse-drawn, open-air buggies, bells softly tinkling, to survey the Khan's vast and neatly planted lands.

The peace and quiet was palpable amid the lush beauty of his carefully cultivated territory. Men and women finished up their day's work in the terraced fields as dusk settled over the fertile green valley.

I was struck by the subtle but pervasive sense of belonging which comes from endless generations living on the same land as their forebears. The collective activity in this tranquil, picturesque valley deeply affected me. The profound sense of enduring community I discerned as the horses clip-clopped past the people walking home along the dirt pathways resonated with my own, as-yet unrecognised yearning for a community bound by work and complex shared ties.

This powerful experience quietly slipped into my subconscious and undoubtedly inspired my decision, months later, to return home and look for meaningful work in Canada.

But for now I was still in Swat, and I would have found it impossible to imagine the horror that would be inflicted on these people some thirty-seven years later by religious extremists ready to forcibly seize control and blow up girls' schools, viciously terrorise women, steal young boys from their families to use as suicide bombers, behead opponents and barbarically hang their bodies to rot in the town square for all to see.

From Swat we drove to Lahore, the second largest city in the country and capital of Punjab province. The trucks and buses on the congested roads, bursting with painted images of Bollywood movie stars, flowers and quotes from famous Pakistani poets and the Qur'an, were even more flamboyant than the Land Rover; but still, our vehicle was a target. The risk for Julie and me of being caught by the police in a vehicle stuffed with hashish was too great and we reluctantly left our American 'drivers' and carried on alone.

Our goal now was to reach India and the beaches of Goa on the coast. It was, we learned from fellow travellers, the mecca for itinerants like us. Anxious to move on, we headed south for Karachi, the capital of Sindh province, ready to catch a boat to Bombay (Mumbai). In Karachi we mingled with the colourful crowds and rummaged through the outdoor bazaars. We selected surprisingly inexpensive, flowing silk chiffon to be stitched into shalwar kameez by the dozens of male tailors perched nearby in the open air on raised wooden platforms, whirring away on their Singer sewing machines. We wore our new outfits with matching scarves, or *dupatta*, wrapped like cowls around our neck or draped loosely over our head.

As a naïve young traveller unaware of the political situation in the country, I assumed, wrongly, that the palpable tension in the air was simply the norm in a country where millions of people live in poverty, rather than the frustrated aftermath of the political turbulence that led to the successful overthrow of one dictator (Ayub Khan), only to be replaced by another (Yahya Khan) and even more political upheaval. Within a year, East Pakistan had won a fierce war with West Pakistan and become the new independent country of Bangladesh. We, however, set sail for India with no clue about the turmoil and upheaval we were leaving behind.

By spring, I was ready to return to Canada after roaming the Delhi and Mumbai markets and the hedonistic hippie scene on the beaches of Goa. Back in Vancouver I found work that replicated, in some ways, the deep sense of community that had so moved me in Swat. Over the next thirty years I helped start and run a co-op radio station, educated students on tenant, women's, labour and other legal rights, became communications director for a public sector trade union, earned a Master's degree in Communication and, after helping win an election, I joined the Office of the Premier of British Columbia as director of strategy and communications. My daughter grew up and began her own travel odyssey.

In a quirk of fate in 2001, a sick friend asked me to take his place at a workshop for political parties in Algeria, organised by a Washington-based non-government organisation – the National Democratic Institute (NDI) chaired by former secretary of state Madeleine Albright. It was the beginning of a fifteen-year stretch living and working in post-conflict countries and developing democracies which, coincidentally, took me back to most of the places I had visited so many years before. My primary purpose was my work but, this time, I soon acquired a passion for the ubiquitous carpets and textiles in the museums, shops and homes I visited.

Based in Skopje, North Macedonia for three years, I travelled from Albania to Zagreb and everywhere in between. Being next door to Turkey allowed weekend trips to Istanbul where I could essay a leisurely wander through the Grand Bazaar, visit Topkapı Palace and discover Elizabeth Hewitt's one-of-a-kind shop in Sultanahmet. My 'textile eye' was opening.

In 2005 I joined the United Nations Development Program to help organise Afghanistan's parliamentary elections. Movement for expats was limited owing to ongoing security threats. But on Fridays I would reserve a jeep and driver to visit the weekend markets with their mounds of vintage goods made by the dizzying array of people – Uzbek, Turkmen, Hazara, Tajik – that streamed into Kabul.[4]

Then I'd head to the same Chicken Street I had visited thirty-five years before, with its still-rickety old wooden shops jammed to the rafters with hand-woven tribal carpets, and striped silk chapans, like the green-and-purple ones worn by President Hamid Karzai. My final stop was at the new boutiques opened by savvy young Afghan women fashion designers who were incorporating vintage textile fragments into contemporary pieces.

One of my American colleagues in Kabul was collecting antique Lakai embroidery. I used to wonder why she was ecstatic each time she found another piece to add to her collection, since I had no idea how unique and rare it was. My exposure to the cornucopia around me was growing exponentially, but my knowledge was still very limited.

In 2006, I took up residence as the Pakistan country director for NDI in Islamabad, in a sprawling two-storey house, surrounded by a towering jacaranda tree, home to lime-green parakeets amid the purple flowers, scented jasmine bushes and a fuchsia bougainvillea-covered wall enclosing the lush green yard. My quest to furnish it took me to a lovely old two-storey home on a nearby street where a tall, lean Turkmen named Ghafur had set up shop. His yard was covered with antique carved wooden doors and window frames, some made into tables, mirrors and picture frames. Inside I saw hand-painted antique furniture, brass and wooden bowls, tribal carpets and embroidered textiles he'd routinely bring back from trips to Central Asia. It was like walking into another century and, to me, it was magical.

Over a period of four years working to strengthen democratic practices with the parliament and political parties, I spent many Sundays, when everything else in the city was closed, at Ghafur's. He would tell me, over bottomless cups of green tea, about the treasures in his shop – Uzbek embroidery, Turkmen chuvals, wooden objects and tribal carpets and kilims. I would usually leave with a carpet or two, or an embroidery, and a slowly growing understanding of what they were.

Carpets and textiles – both old and new – became a big part of my life in Pakistan, with its centuries-old weaving and embroidery traditions[5] and where new textile production is one of the most vital sectors of the economy. Thousands of shops and markets sell fabric to a population who, largely, still have their clothing stitched by a tailor.

My tailor would come to my home, take my measurements and return with the clothing, drapery or upholstery I had ordered just days earlier. The only glitch was zippers. Since traditional Pakistani clothing does not use them, installing zippers in the Western-style pants I preferred was a challenge never quite mastered.

Shopping was a most pleasant experience, as shopkeepers would often offer biscuits and tea to sip while they displayed their goods. I loved to peruse the vast selection of khadi cloth, block-printed cotton, tie and dyed silk, intricately embroidered and hand-beaded fabric, kurtas and dupattas as well as the finest plain, plaid and pinstriped wool suiting found in the 'men's' sections.

Maharajah, owned by some Jain brothers, was a large shop in the area officially named Super Market. It proved to be a delightful source of tribal carpets and all kinds of textile, new and old. The selection of hand-embroidered Kashmir shawls was the best in the city,[6] and it was there that I sunk my hand, for the first time, into a shahtoosh pashmina made from the buttery hair of the chiru, a now-endangered species of goat.

Jinnah Market, a bustling outdoor mall within walking distance from my house, was a constant source of amusement with shops that spanned the low to high ends of the spectrum. Besides precious gems and sparkling gold jewellery, there were dozens of shops selling brightly coloured and boldly patterned cotton and silk textiles, intricately carved wood furniture, blood-red Turkmen and dark-blue Baluch carpets from Afghanistan, finely embroidered Kashmiri wool shawls and paper-thin pashminas, cheap imported goods from China, and turquoise ceramics from Iran. Outdoor food stalls sold freshly squeezed mango and pomegranate juice and savoury snacks like samosa, pakora and 'chat', stands crackling with the sound and smell of roasting popcorn. Of the mouth-watering sweets like jalebi and burfi, my favourite was carrot halwa.

Jinnah Market also housed Herat Carpets, one of the better carpet shops in town, owned by an elderly Afghan man and run by his four sons. Their finest and biggest carpets were kept in their home, where I fell in love with Beshir examples among the many other Turkmen carpets on display.

One of my favourite trips was to Peshawar, the capital of the North West Frontier Province, where the Afghan Market was located, which I visited frequently until it became too dangerous due to violent attacks by extremists. The market was housed in a dark and crumbling three-storey building packed with dozens of small shops and stalls selling handmade blue and green glass from Herat, silver Kuchi and Turkmen jewellery, lapis lazuli, embroidered textiles, and fine beadwork on naturally dyed textiles. I bought several rare pieces of the delicate embroidery for which Swat is famous.

Driving through Peshawar to the market in the old town was always an adventure. Staring out the window I saw a sinewy elderly man running alongside our vehicle pulling a big wooden cart piled high with freshly skinned cows, their wide open eyes staring me in the face. Overhead a thick web of dozens of entangled, exposed electrical wires crisscrossed the street in an intricate jerry-rigged network to redirect the flow from one source to another.

The winding narrow dirt streets around the Afghan Market were crowded with goats, trucks, donkey-drawn carts and people all struggling to inch forward in the chaos. The decrepit, precariously leaning two-

and three-storey buildings, dating back a couple of centuries with their ornately carved wood balconies, were poised to collapse.

Sadly, since my first trip to the city decades earlier, hundreds of thousands of Afghan refugees had fled to the city from the conflict and war in their own neighbouring country.

As I travelled around the vast, diverse country, there was always somewhere to see beautiful carpets and textiles, even when security was tight. I was once staying in the heavily guarded Serena Hotel in Quetta, the capital of the province of Baluchistan, known equally for its woven wool carpets and an ongoing insurgency; a large embroidered textile in the hotel shop caught my eye. It was, surprisingly, an old Uzbek suzani, although at the time I thought it was a local piece. I bought it along with a beat-up old carpet which turned out to be just a beat-up old carpet, but I still have the suzani. My 'eye' was improving, if slowly.

I left Pakistan in 2010. During my four years, the country had been through violent political upheaval. Benazir Bhutto – the first and only elected female leader of a country with a majority Muslim population – had been assassinated, and the parliament had peacefully overthrown a military dictator and rid the constitution of undemocratic clauses imposed by dictators.

After I returned to North America, I longed to keep alive my experience from the other side of the world. Carpets and textiles became a way to stay connected through the rich legacy inspired and initiated by the people on the pages of this book, and other people like them, by organisations, conferences, courses, fairs, tours and publications.[7]

In 2010 I took my first rug- and textile-focused trip to Sweden for the International Conference of Oriental Carpets[8] which included a trip to St Petersburg where we had access to the city's magnificent museums and their Central Asian antique treasures. When I moved to New York in 2012, I was excited to discover the monthly talks sponsored by the Hajji Baba Club,[9] the oldest rug society in North America. Walking the streets of my Brooklyn neighbourhood I stumbled on Kea Carpets and Kilims, where I could reminisce with Susan Gomersall[10] about the good old days in Peshawar. ABC Carpet & Home[11] was where I went to daydream, as I roamed its six floors of impeccably curated textiles, carpets and other treasures from South Asia.

In 2017, when I was in London for a course on Indian textiles at the Victoria and Albert Museum, I was thrilled to visit Pip Rau's house, which was bursting with rare textiles on ikat- and suzani-covered walls, Joss Graham's exquisite shop of handmade treasures, John Gillow's exuberant booth at a fair and Steven Cohen's extraordinary collection of Katawaz bags.[12]

When Ben Evans and Rachel Meek from HALI magazine[13] asked me to write a piece about what I had seen, I realised there was a bigger story to tell about these people, and others, who had travelled from Turkey to India and fallen in love with the profusion of textiles and carpets they saw in the markets and streets along the way. Unlike me, and most of the other travellers on the hippie trail, these discerning individuals were seduced by the colour and distinctive craft they saw and began to accumulate a critical mass of material that soon appealed to collectors, galleries, interior designers and museums back in their home countries.

Over decades of visits, they established networks of 'pickers' and local dealers who found and sold them the oldest, most beautiful, or technically interesting antique and vintage textiles of their kind gleaned from otherwise inaccessible villages and private homes. Some decided to explore their new-found interest professionally, becoming academics, museum curators and noted experts. Others pursued their obsession by becoming dealers in places like New York, London, Santa Fe, Toronto and elsewhere, where they established unique shops that showcased their latest finds.

Not all these enterprises lasted. But some endured through the decades and provided the opportunity for many people to see and learn about handmade indigenous textiles and carpets from cultures and places they had never been to and never heard of. The new interest fostered by these carpet and textile pioneers produced keen collectors, fresh research and dozens of books to feed the growing interest of the enthusiasts they had generated. Their research, books, and some of the rare private collections they assembled over time, are a lasting contribution to the fields of ethnography, anthropology, textile studies, cultural studies, museology, history, interior design, popular culture and fashion.

Today, indigenous designs and motifs from these far-off countries have penetrated our collective consciousness. They can be found everywhere from haute couture[14] to high-end interior design studios[15] to the mass marketing of Indian block-printed bedding, tableware and clothing in stores like Walmart.

The dealers and collectors who spent their lives seeking these complex pieces of the past have intriguing stories to tell and collections of some of the finest embroidery, weaving and other global textiles of their kind in the world. Their individual stories are alive with passion, adventure and a willingness to follow their instincts. Taken together, they are an enlightening guide to understanding how we connect to the past, and how textiles connect the world.

1   Some of the funding/programmes included: US Government: Peace Corps, Head Start; Canadian Government: Canada Council, Company of Young Canadians, Local Initiatives Program, Opportunities for Youth, Non-Medical Use of Drugs Directorate; UK Government: British Council Grants; etc.

2   MacLean, *Magic Bus: On the Hippie Trail from Istanbul to India*, p. 38.

3   The NWFP is now called Khyber Pakhtunkhwa.

4   See Steven Cohen, p. 182, Andy Hale, p. 144, Kate Fitz Gibbon, p. 166 and Pip Rau, p. 42.

5   See Joss Graham, p. 18, John Gillow, p. 126, and Susan Gomersall, p. 106.

6   See Frank Ames, p. 64.

7   The International Conference on Oriental Carpets; HALI magazine and other publications; HALI Tours with behind-the-scene visits to museums and private collections, plus other expert-guided textile tours; rug societies like the New York Hajji Baba Club; books written by collectors.

8   ICOC, http://www.icoc-orientalrugs.org/

9   Hajji Baba Club, www.hajjibaba.org

10 See Susan Gomersall, p. 106.

11 See Connecting the world: Designers and influencers, p. 202.

12 See Joss Graham, p. 18, Pip Rau, p. 42, John Gillow, p. 126, and Steven Cohen, p. 182.

13 HALI magazine, established in 1978, is an international magazine published four times per year, covering the textile arts of all cultures and periods, www.hali.com

14 Yves Saint Laurent's famous collection of silk ikat prints from Uzbekistan; see Elizabeth Hewitt, pp. 86.

15 See Connecting the world: Designers and influencers, p. 202.

CROATIA

RUSSIA

NORTH MACEDONIA
• Skopje

GREECE

Island of Crete

• Ayvalık
Bursa •
• Istanbul

TURKEY

Mount Ararat •

UZBEKISTAN
• Tashkent

• Tehran

• Mashad

IRAN

Balkh •
Tashkurgan
Kunduz
Aqcha •
• Mazar-i-Sharif
Herat •
Khyber Pakhtunkhwa
Baba Sadiq •
Kohistan
AFGHANISTAN
Kabul •
Jalalabad •
Swat
• Mingora
Khyber Pass
Peshawar •
• Islamabad
Kandahar •

Quetta •
• Lahore
PAKISTAN
• Bahawalpur
Punjab
• Najibabad
Baluchistan
Rajasthan
• Delhi
Sindh
Umerkot •
Thar Desert
Karachi •
• Chachro
INDIA

Gujarat

Ajanta caves •

• Mumbai

GREECE

• Athens

Island of Lesvos
Island of Kea
Molyvos •

Island of Crete

Goa

• Heraklion
Matala caves •

**Places of note on the travels
of the people portrayed in these pages**

• Kochi

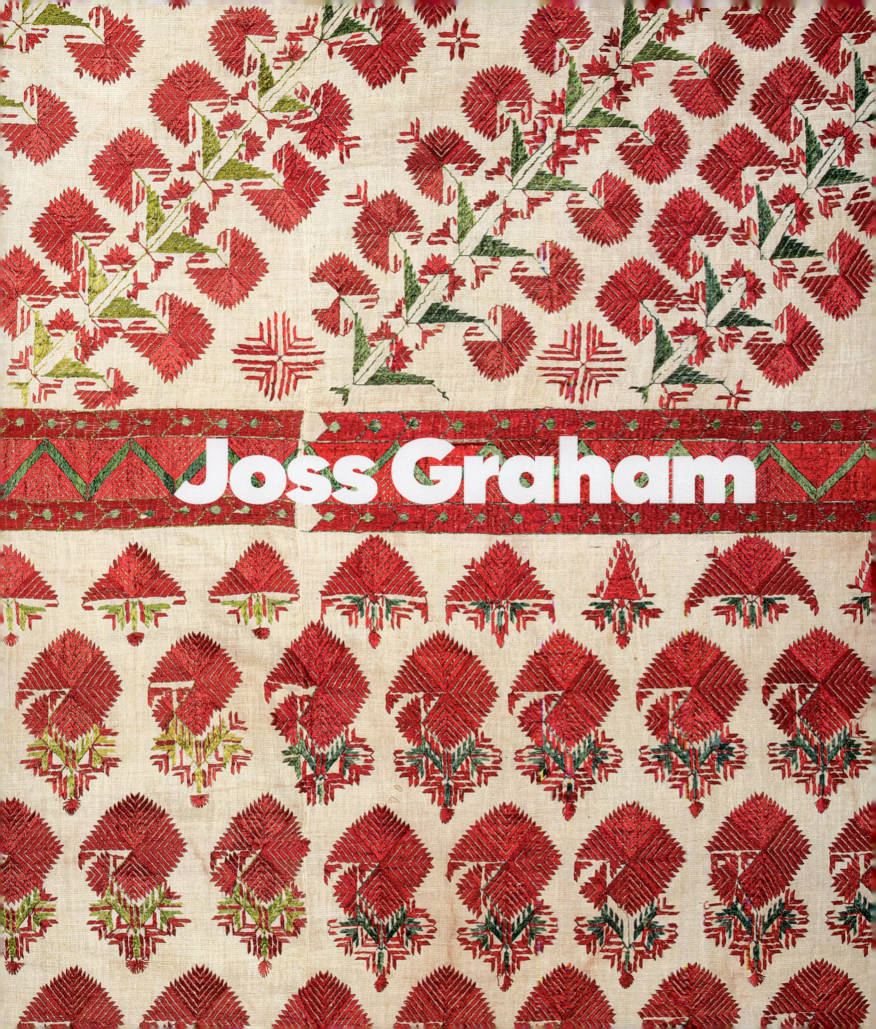

Joss Graham

Striking out on his own

It was in 1970, during his first trip to India, that Joss Graham encountered an unforgettable scene involving the Banjara – one of the country's most fascinating communities, renowned for their intricately embroidered mirror-work, elaborate silver jewellery and colourful attire. 'I had spent the day at Ajanta, the Buddhist caves. I had become immersed in the visual splendour of the extraordinary frescoes. When I came down I jumped on a bus back to the railway station. There were a couple of young Banjara men on the seat opposite me wearing a long scarf around both their heads, singing antiphonally. They were peeling oranges and shooting the juice from the peel up their noses and singing. It was like watching a Fellini movie, and I was in it.'

The experience captured his imagination and helps explain why India has remained a central focus of his life ever since. Over the succeeding years he 'would collect many rare textiles from the Banjara.' However, back in 1970 he had no idea that he would open a shop, become a prominent textile dealer and collector, and supply many top-level museums around the world with exceptional textiles from South Asia.

The family background exposed him from an early age to stories of travel and life in far-away cultures and countries. His paternal grandparents had been in the colonial service in Egypt, living on a houseboat on the Nile opposite the exclusive Gezira Club, which opened in 1882. When the weather became warm in Egypt they would migrate back to Scotland, taking a boat from Alexandria to Venice and the Orient Express to Paris, crossing over to England and making their way up to Perthshire for the season; then in the autumn the family would journey all the way back to Egypt for the

opener
Detail of a thirma bagh, northern Punjab,
Pakistan, circa 1875, Joss Graham collection
left
Joss Graham in his shop in London
above
Flatweaves in Joss Graham's London shop

Photo: Monica Fritz

winter. Walter Harris, the famous *Times* correspondent based in Tangier, was Joss Graham's great uncle and shared the same birthday. Gavin Maxwell's book *Lords of the Atlas*, based on Walter Harris's life and career in Morocco, had recently been published. 'I wanted to live a life like him,' says Graham.

After he left Winchester College, in 1968 a volunteer post in Addis Ababa led to a year in Ethiopia, teaching in the Asere Hawariat school, followed by going up to read archaeology and anthropology at Cambridge University. In his second year he switched to social anthropology. 'I liked the idea of studying a living culture. Cultural relativism was part of the 1960s zeitgeist,' he says. A phrase he heard in use at the time still intrigues him: 'The earth grows a different kind of human every hundred miles.' As he puts it in his own words, 'You've only got to travel a bit and you come across a different way of being – there's a palpable difference in culture, and it's even more true the further afield you go.'

Antonia Graham, his older sister, had already travelled widely, so on his university summer break Graham decided to emulate her adventures and take off for India. Hitch hiking alone from London, he slept in a ditch outside a police station in Greece and took buses across Turkey, sleeping in cheap hotels. An especially bad one underneath Mount Ararat remains an uneasy memory. 'The room was the smallest possible and it was infested with every kind of insect you might imagine. I don't know why I put up with it. But you just fell out of the bus and had to lay your head down somewhere, and that was it.'

He rode on the top of the front of a truck through the Khyber Pass from Afghanistan down to Peshawar, Pakistan and up into Swat and Kalam – his route into northwest Pakistan and the tribal areas. 'It was a bit like the highlands of Scotland – water running in channels everywhere and statuesque deodar pine trees,' he says, though the black-turbaned men with hennaed orange beards were a notable difference.

Graham was travelling, like many others at the time, as part of a spiritual quest. Once he reached India, he pursued his interest in religion, venturing up to the holy city of Rishikesh in the Himalayan foothills, where he volunteered in an ashram in exchange for chapatis and dal. His job at the ashram was to haul uprooted trees from the Ganges, a river worshipped as the young and powerful goddess Ganga, and deposit them in the kitchen storeroom so they could be chopped up for firewood. It was the monsoon and the river was in flood, with trees cartwheeling in the turbulence. He recalls a talk by the Maharishi Mahesh Yogi, the Indian yoga guru who introduced transcendental meditation to the Beatles among many others. The fireflies in the orchard illuminated the darkness.

On a later trip, he was fortunate to practise yoga under B. K. S. Iyengar, one of the foremost yoga teachers in the world at that time. At his early

above
Joss Graham at the Ajanta
Caves, India, 1973
opposite
Family group, Jaisalmer District,
Rajasthan, 1976, photographed
by Joss Graham

above
Blouse front, Lohana group, commissioned
from Meghwal embroiderers, Kutch, early
20th century, Nasreen Askari and The Hasan
A. Foundation, Karachi
opposite
Recycled quilted cotton goderi (dowry textile),
Saami Fakir mendicants, Lower Sindh,
Pakistan, circa 1950

morning classes Iyengar would talk about how you should feel and how the body should behave during the asanas. 'When I came out of classes with him I swear that I could see 360 degrees. He was the most inspiring teacher.' Later still, introduced to the Vipassana school of meditation, he took a ten-day course at a residential meditation centre in Igatpuri in the Western Ghats with S. N. Goenka, the well-known Indian teacher of Vipassana meditation whose classes attracted hundreds of people from around the world. 'He taught me the benefits of *meta* or self-compassion before practising the giving of compassion to others.'

Back in London after his eight weeks of travel through Turkey, Iran, Afghanistan, Pakistan and India, it was all a bit of a blur. His mother told him he came back with two full suitcases – one containing miniature paintings he'd bought in Delhi and the other stuffed with textiles. 'I remember buying the paintings but I don't recall the circumstances of acquiring the textiles at all. They were likely purchased from the Wagris on the footpaths lining Janpath in New Delhi.'

Around a year later, he took the suitcases to show John Irwin, then the keeper of the Indian Department at London's Victoria and Albert Museum. Explaining that he wanted to continue travelling back and forth to India, he asked which would be better to bring back to sell – miniature paintings or textiles? Irwin told him he should 'stick to textiles because there was no restriction in taking them out of the country, whereas miniature paintings

above
Embroidered gaj (blouse neck panel), Talpur royal family, Hyderabad, Sindh, Pakistan, ca. 1880, Shireen Feroze Nana collection
opposite
Refugee camp, Barmer District, Rajasthan, 1976, photographed by Joss Graham

are subject to export laws and regulations'. Serendipity had set Graham on a path, but at that moment he was unaware of it. It would take another trip to India, with his sister, and an unexpected phone call after his return to London, before everything came into perspective.

Graham had met Faith and John Singh in Jaipur where they had started Anokhi,[2] a clothing company which has since become internationally recognised as a byword for Indian printed textiles. They had recently acquired a substantial collection of embroidered textiles purchased from Hindu refugees, principally the Meghwal community, who had been displaced from Pakistan to India because of the 1971 war between the two countries.[3] After hostilities ceased, the Hindus living on the Pakistani side of the Thar Desert in the province of Sindh were obliged to migrate to nearby Rajasthan on the Indian side while the Muslim castes and other communities remained on the Pakistan side.

Anokhi had acquired these textiles for design ideas, buying from the refugees who were selling them to help get re-established. John and Faith had bought far more than they needed, to try to help the refugees, and had shipped the excess to London; but these embroideries were not wanted by any of the shops they supplied. Faith and her brother, Luke, called Graham to see if he would handle their sale, as they knew he was already dealing in Indian textiles. After he said yes, a van arrived at the 18th-century squat in King's Cross where he was living and deposited a three-foot pile of textiles on his floor.

Rather than immediately trying to sell this collection, Graham had a different idea. He had started a post-graduate degree programme, but it hadn't gone well because he lacked a focus. As soon as this huge quantity of textiles arrived he suddenly knew that they were a perfect subject for anthropological study. 'I had all the representative material I might possibly want,' he says.

The first step was to identify exactly what the textiles were. There were many pieces that were similar in shape, design and technique; and, after a while, he understood what they were. 'I was informed that a young woman, in preparation for her marriage, will stitch pieces of a blouse – the embroidered portion for the chest and sleeves. After marriage, she will attach her choice of printed or tie-dyed cotton, make a neck fastening, and she has a beautiful blouse to wear.'

Soon after the textiles were delivered Graham flew, in 1975, to Karachi, the capital of the southern province of Sindh, to learn more about these embroideries in the place where they had originated. It proved to be an excellent decision. 'As soon as I arrived there were

lots of people willing and able to tell me and show me.' He met many of the people in Pakistan who were interested in textiles at that time, he says, acknowledging his good fortune.

He had an introduction to Shireen Feroze Nana who, he had been told, was the person to see. Shireen, hailing from a noble family of Persian and Georgian ancestry, was married to a distinguished judge of the Sindh High Court from a Parsee family.[4] Every three months they used to make a round trip to the capitals of the country's four provinces,[5] where Justice Nana held circuit court sessions and where she would meet all the local dignitaries. She used those trips as a way to collect and study the various traditions of embroidery.

'Shireen taught me an enormous amount,' Joss says, crediting her with starting him off on the study of embroidery and textiles from Sindh. She introduced him to Dr Harchand Rai, a well-known Hindu doctor in Umerkot, a town in the Thar Desert, who took Graham under his wing. He travelled to places in the desert that had been thriving towns but were abandoned when the army passed through and the

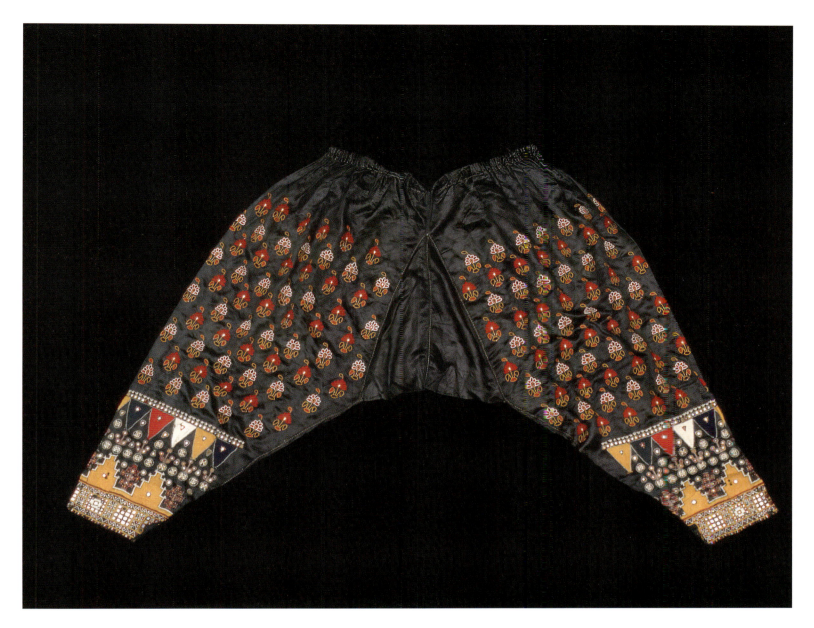

Hindus had to flee to India. 'They took with them whatever portable possessions they could, which were embroideries, the most important things they still had,' he says. 'Back in Karachi Shireen showed me her collection and sent me to visit other collectors and the few dealers in the bazaar who sold them.'

He learned that the kind of pieces Anokhi had shipped him were made by both Hindu and Muslim communities before Partition in 1947. 'They were not made for sale. They were made by people for their own use and the artistry was amazing,' he says.

The textiles, Graham learned on these travels, serve more than one purpose. The embroidery is subject to a kind of cultural competition where the social status of the family is measured by the accomplishment and quantity of the work. A young girl is expected, as part of her dowry, to have assembled a trosseau of embroidered outfits by the time she gets married. There was an identifiable hierarchy of design and execution. 'The embroidery of the very highest Muslim community, Sayyids [descendants of the Prophet], was finer and more delicate than that of any other community,' he says. 'The needlework on the fronts of the aba [shortsleeved long dresses worn by women] produced by the Sayyids of Kutch and Lower Sindh is breath-taking. The strong light of the desert helped the women to stitch incredibly fine work.'

The embroideries of Sindh led Graham to take a different tack from that of most other Western travellers at the time, who were more enamoured with Afghanistan and India. A fascination grew with this particular area of southern Pakistan on the Indian Ocean where other Westerners weren't travelling. Most of the carpet and textile dealers were located in Peshawar, a town in northwestern Pakistan close to the Afghan border. Few had ventured as far south as Karachi, a city which appealed to Graham for its diversity of people. 'You could walk around the bazaars and meet Turkmens and Uzbeks with their carpets, as well as Afghan and Baluch tribesmen, alongside Hindu traders, Jogi snake charmers and Saami Fakir, as well as the faithful en route to Mecca on the Haj pilgrimage,' he says. 'I struck out on my own by going to Pakistan, and as long as Shireen Feroze Nana was alive, she was my first port of call.' Shireen eventually divided her collection between her six children and also, with Graham's assistance, the Victoria and Albert Museum.

Visiting Pakistan in each of the next five or six years, Graham continued to explore places off the beaten track and meet more remarkable characters. The country was experiencing a political crackdown at the time under the brutal dictator Muhammad Zia-ul-Haq (in power 1977–88), who had orchestrated the non-judicial hanging in 1979 of Zulfikar Ali Bhutto, the first democratically elected prime minister. However, 'I didn't come across any of that kind of political tension in Pakistan,' he says, noting that he was able to go anywhere he wanted despite the political conditions in the country.

One of the characters he met was Jerry Anderson, part Scottish and part Pakistani, who travelled around Pakistan's remote western province of Baluchistan trapping snakes and animals which he sold to zoos, and collecting Baluch rugs and flatweaves. He was the source of the rugs detailed in the ground-breaking *Textiles of Baluchistan* by M. G. Konieczny.

'Jerry was a wild man and drank a fierce amount. The Baluch chiefs thought of him as a finishing school for their sons. If you went to visit him you would always meet inebriated youth. It was very difficult to remember the next day anything this man had told you, since the amount of whisky drunk was so large.' Anderson kept snakes and wild animals in pens in his courtyard. 'Once I visited and there was an incredibly rare round-eyed cat living on top of a stinking pile of Baluch rugs soaked in urine.'

Despite his colourful antics, Anderson had a deep knowledge of the area. He knew how the various cultural traditions and influences had travelled from Samarkand, Kabul and elsewhere down through the northern passes, eventually establishing the Mughal Empire. The second important pathway into Pakistan was the Makran Corridor along the shores of the Indian Ocean from Iran. People, techniques and ideas travelled along this coast, mostly by boat, as part of the great Indian Ocean trade. Dhows used to ply this route travelling from Sri Lanka up the coast of Western India and round to Iran and the Gulf, before continuing to Mombasa and Zanzibar. The patterns of the kilims of the Qashqa'i and Luri reappear in the ralli quilts of Sindh. Other migrations and influences, Anderson recounted, travelled in the opposite direction, such as the Roma[6] who broke off from the Banjara peoples in India around 1000 CE and travelled west into Europe and North Africa.

Through these discussions, Anderson helped map out, for Graham, the connections visible in the textiles. 'The embroidery of Syria and the embroidery of certain Baluch tribes are similar because they're actually the same people, due to the fact that animal grazing moved them great distances over a period of a few hundred years.'[7] Motifs, stitches, styles of embroidery and belief systems travel from one place to another, something that resonated with Graham's studies in anthropology. 'The ethno-history is complex and fascinated me,' he says.

In between trips to Pakistan, Graham organised an exhibition, 'The Flowering Sand', at the Textural Art Gallery in London in 1977, showcasing the Thar Desert pieces he had received from Anokhi. He put them on as an art show because he thought their beauty was worthy of admiration and that they should be seen as a comprehensive collection. 'I picked the ones that I thought were the best quality. It's obviously a thin line between what appeals to you personally, and publicly exhibiting them as art.' He sold a lot of the pieces to embroidery collectors in England and abroad, he says, adding that's where he met some of his current collector clients. Good coverage in the *Observer* colour supplement helped launch a career specialising in textiles from a region that remains central to his collection.

The 'hippie era' had almost come to an end, but there were still some shops in London selling 'flower power': colourful ikat, suzanis, embroidered dresses and other textiles and rugs from Afghanistan. There were boutiques, like Forbidden Fruit on the Portobello Road,

opposite
Abochchani wedding shawl, Upper Sindh, Pakistan, 19th century, private collection

Pip Rau on Islington Green and Oxus, the famous but short-lived gallery on Langton Street off the King's Road in Chelsea. Graham began to sell his pieces to shops like Conran and the General Trading Company.

Most other travellers didn't own shops and sold, instead, from stalls they had in various markets. Graham did open a shop in 1980, mainly because a great opportunity came up. His first wife and her business partner had decided to vacate their premises and move their kilim business to Chelsea Green. Graham moved into the shop on Eccleston Street in Central London's upmarket district of Belgravia, where the business remains today.

Having a shop has tied him down but it's also given him a platform from which to work. He expanded the repertoire of Pakistani embroidered textiles he had received from Anokhi to include other handmade textiles sourced on trips to Pakistan and India, as well as to Turkey, Syria, Morocco and sub-Saharan Africa. Together with the embroideries, many other textiles and associated crafts became part of the inventory, principally wood-block printing, tie dye and ikat. Another fundamental change was the inclusion of jewellery and other crafts found in these same cultures, such as pottery, woodcarving and baskets. 'I am attracted to stones and metallurgy. Jewellery and textiles are first cousins.'

'I've always been fascinated by people who make things,' he says, attributing this to his engineer father, Brigadier Peter Graham, a ballistics expert, who had pursued a career designing shells and rifling for the UK's Centurian battle tank. 'He was always making things – from musical instruments to a man-powered glider which never got off the ground.'

What Graham really likes is 'the touch of the hand', which he thinks is also appealing to his customers and accounts for the universal appreciation of hand-spun, hand-woven textiles, whether cotton or other traditional natural fibres. 'There is a palpable difference when something is made by hand.'

Textiles interest him most in terms of their tactile and visual beauty expressed in the material, technique, motifs and designs, 'But if you have to pay the rent you have to sell things that the general public wants, otherwise you'll be out of business.' Other shops started to introduce cheaper machine-made alternatives which simulate the 'look' of authentic materials. 'Fortunately there has been and continues to be a growing appreciation for other cultures and their unique textile and craft traditions which has sustained me these forty-or-so years.'

Listening to him talk about textiles, however, it's clear where his passion lies. 'The thing I really like about textiles is their texture and sheen and even smell. It's kind of an abstract thing to do with material, the softness of cotton, the sheen of silk and the lustre of wool, the power and beauty of colour. They're part of nature and one of humanity's greatest achievements,' he says, 'because we've managed to improve upon nature by making all these textiles based on natural materials but shaped and perfected by us.'

Photo: Monica Fritz

above
Detail of an abochchani, Upper Sindh, Pakistan, circa 1900, private collection
opposite
Shi'a Hazara rumal, Afghanistan, circa 1850, private collection

Graham continued to travel frequently after he opened the shop, patiently pursuing his interest in textiles and the cultures that produce them. He has never been happy buying items in the villages because inevitably, he says, the person you're buying from is thrust into the spotlight. There may be jealousy, or condemnation. He emphasises the need for an outsider to show sensitivity when entering a small community. 'That person you're buying from is almost certainly going to ask you a high price because they might lose face if word gets out that they sold it for too little.' His approach was always to go in as a visitor, sometimes a guest, who is interested in knowing what's what. 'It's rather intrusive, thinking that we can travel around and visit these villages and poke into what they're doing. As an anthropologist you can somehow rationalise it, but otherwise it is very difficult.'

Being a man has posed further challenges. 'I came back from one trip realising that I couldn't get any reliable information,' he says. As a man, he couldn't meet the women who did the embroidery. Acknowledging the need to have female assistance, he advertised in a newspaper in London and interviewed more than a dozen women to find a suitable female companion to accompany him on his next trip. He chose a Polish 'Sarmatian' and her four-year-old daughter, and the sixty-year-old English photographer and surrealist artist Stella Snead, who had lived in Mumbai. Arriving in a jeep in a rural village, they appeared to the locals as a family of a mother, husband, wife, daughter, and their interpreter.

Graham would drive and stand by the jeep, polishing the windscreen. Slowly, the villagers opened their doors. Thanks to acquaintance being made in such a way, the local people were far friendlier, he had much better entrée and, he says, 'We ate delicious food and were able to gain greater insight into the role of textiles in the lives of the people.'

Over the next several years, Graham shifted his focus to India, where the textile traditions in Gujarat and Rajasthan are incredibly rich and very closely related, not surprisingly, to those in Sindh, Pakistan. Before the 1947 Partition of the two countries people could easily cross back and forth.

'I would go to India about once a year on a sourcing trip. My interest in certain tribes and their work – mainly things that I thought were special or were made using a particular technique – determined where I went and what I collected, which often meant discovering the obscure and unusual. I've always been keen on Banjara embroidery and have a big collection of it.' Although the embroideries were little known at the time, he recognised the unique quality of the brilliant colours, elaborate embroidery and exquisite mirror-work which incorporates cotton, silk, wool, fibre, cowries, mirrors, base metals and tassels.

Dhurrie rugs were another early favourite. They have been woven for generations by men, and more recently by women in the villages of northern India as part of the trousseau to take to their future home. They were also made commercially by male weavers, notably in the prisons of British India. Flatwoven cotton bridal dhurries provide a picture of contemporary rural life in Punjab. As women were reluctant to part with them, they were largely unknown at the time, outside the area where they were woven.[8]

He learned about kantha quilting and embroidery from Bengal from dealers in Delhi who had textiles from every region of India. Good Bengali kanthas have almost disappeared from the market, but when he first went to Delhi there were excellent pieces available. The V&A purchased the first two pieces he brought back. He went to Bengal to explore, characteristically heading to the original source to learn as much as he could about where and how they were made and used. In this way he went to the Ashutosh Museum of Indian Art and Kalighat, West Bengal, to meet Buddha Bhai, a famous Vagri[9] dealer.

The pursuit of specific textiles was rarely straightforward and required a good eye, as they were not always found where they were expected to be. 'I was introduced to a hawker who brought me some kanthas. When she opened her bundle there wasn't anything worthy of my attention inside, but then I noticed that the bundle itself had been wrapped in a very interesting kantha. That was just a chance thing of realising that the treasure was the wrapper. Krishna Riboud purchased this piece, which was illustrated on the poster for the exhibition 'Woven Air: The Muslin and Kantha Tradition of Bangladesh' at the Whitechapel Art Gallery in 1988.

For Graham, it was important not only to sell the textiles he sourced, but also to share with others what he had seen and learned. After returning from his travels, he would organise an exhibition in his shop of what he had collected along with whatever else he could add that was pertinent, garnered from friends, auction houses and fellow dealers. 'I think that's one of the things dealers do. If they're interested in something they just amass similar pieces and information from other people.'

He held a seminar on Banjara embroidery, where he invited various collectors to 'show and tell' some of their pieces, even though few knew much about them; they just liked them. This coincided with the launch for a new book, *Textiles of the Banjara: Cloth and Culture of a Wandering Tribe*, by Charlotte Kwon and Tim McLaughlin, which includes several pieces from his collection.[10]

Some people really don't care what the story is behind an object, he admits, it's just something beautiful and they'll buy it. Other people like to be told a story about its origins. He sets great value on talks and exhibitions for collectors and interested observers.

In the beginning, his customers were buying pieces for decoration. Many had travelled to India and were doing their houses up with an Indian touch. Because he was collecting what was available at the time, a lot of it was not particularly old – it had been made one or two generations previously. It's only more recently that he has been able to afford or even find some of the more historical pieces that are hundreds of years old, because Mughal textiles have never been freely available. 'You don't just get lucky and walk into a market in Delhi and find a fragment of a Mughal carpet,' he says.

After amassing large collections of pieces that were rare, like the kantha and Banjara, he introduced them over the years to museums. Various collectors with whom he has dealt have exhibited the textiles in galleries and museums and published books about them.

Graham always had a few collectors who would take the crème de la crème. One of them was the aforementioned Krishna Riboud, a charismatic Bengali art collector who had a legendary private textile museum in Paris, AEDTA, and who purchased regularly from him. 'She enjoyed them in a similar way to how I enjoyed them, spreading them over the sofas of her London apartment,' he says. After she died her granddaughter donated her collection, including her Indian collections, to the Musée Guimet in Paris.

Other textiles of his have ended up in similarly high-profile museums. When he first started exhibiting Banjara material in the shop, he sold a quantity of pieces to the Victoria and Albert Museum. Robert Skelton, successor to John Irwin, was fascinated by the abstract geometric patterns which were the language of design predominant in India before the Mughal era.

Another celebrated curator, Richard Blurton, collected extensively for the British Museum. In this way the museum built up a small collection of kantha masterpieces from a time when they were still available.

Graham also used the shop to offer workshops on specific techniques, led by artisans like British weaver Peter Collingwood who gave a masterclass one year on ply-split braiding. Another time his fondness for West African textiles led him to invite Nike Davies-Okundaye, the iconic indigo dyer from Nigeria, to bring the raw materials necessary to make indigo dye and to conduct workshops. 'We had an indigo vat running for about three months in the yard at the back of the shop. People could come for a day and dye whatever they liked.' The workshops brought him in touch with experts such as indigo specialist Jenny Balfour-Paul, whom he credits with introducing him to indigo-dyed textiles from many other parts of the world like Yemen, Tunisia and Senegal.

A fascination with the migration of patterns, ideas and designs, coupled with his inherent curiosity, took Graham further afield to Syria, Morocco, Afghanistan, Turkey and Tibet. More recently, he has been to Mexico, Armenia, Georgia, Bali and Australia. Although he loves to travel, he is reluctant to claim he understands everywhere he's been. 'I think you can't get under the skin of somewhere that easily. You can start to feel very comfortable and believe you can pick up all the signals and make sense of the language, but it's very difficult to absorb the mindset of another place.'

There is at least one place he can claim to understand, even if he didn't plan it when he started his travels there more than fifty years ago: India has been the country he's always gone back to, and he has seen it in every season and at all times of the day and night. 'Most people fascinated by textiles are interested in a lot of places, but there's usually one that they return to.'

There have been profound changes from the days Graham first travelled in the Indian subcontinent. In a deserted village in Sindh, he met an elderly woman sitting in a doctor's waiting room turning her summer quilt into a winter quilt by patiently adding layers. 'Do you realise that this village has ninety-two PhDs in North America?' she asked him. Forty years beforehand, she explained, everybody had left and gone to New York and Ontario to study. Now they were successful doctors and lawyers. 'What have they left behind?' she questioned.

This was a village that had a tradition of highly skilled and individual embroidery from the Memon community 100 years ago, but now there is little trace of it because nearly everybody has moved away. They weren't forced out, they just saw an opportunity for a better life and were able to travel. 'Still,' says Graham, 'one feels a little guilty that some of these communities have been pressured by modern life into selling their heirlooms. Their remaining descendants are now living with plastic in a desert with no tangible ancestral inheritance to accompany them.'

It is not just people who have left India behind. In the same past 100 years a vast amount of cultural material has travelled into Western Europe and North America. 'I'm not raising the spectre of cultural appropriation, although some people today might blame colonialism. India has always had a mercantile culture, it has always attracted travellers and traders. It was the centre of a huge network for luxury and utility fabrics being shipped to the Middle East, the

Mediterranean, Africa and Asia for centuries before European merchants arrived in 1498. By the 18th century, Indian makers were responding to demands from as far away as Holland and the Americas.'

Nonetheless it saddens him profoundly that many of the poorer Indian people, who were brought up with handmade things, are now unable to afford a cotton sari and have to be satisfied with a polyester one made in China. 'That seems totally wrong,' he says.

While he loves and collects the old pieces, he also has high regard for the textiles and handicrafts being made today. He sells many contemporary textiles and garments from India because the standard is high and they don't have to be incredibly expensive. Recently he has specialised in the production of Brigitte Singh's blockprinted textiles from Amber, Rajasthan. A production of made-to-measure bamboo 'chik' blinds from Delhi, with designs based on

Mughal *jaalis* (latticed screens) now plays an equal part in his business. Commissioning high-quality craft helps ensure the continuity of tradition and the perpetuation of livelihood.

Another current project he has undertaken is writing a catalogue for a private Italian collection of phulkaris, an embroidered shawl with floral designs and other geometrical shapes made using silk thread. This project makes clear that, after decades of collecting, research and travel, his passion in learning about textiles has not diminished. 'The phulkari tradition stretches all the way from the mountains of Pakistan down through Punjab, its epicentre, to Delhi, and there are significant and telling variations in different geographical locations.'

In the forty years since he first opened his shop Graham has noticed little difference in the type of people coming in. 'I can get three generations of the same family in the shop at the same time – grandma, mum and daughter – and they're all just as interested.' He also gets many visitors who are first- or second-generation South Asians living in the UK, whose parents or grandparents came to live in London or the north of England. 'They appreciate being able to see the things their parents or grandparents made and enjoyed.

'People like to collect, it's timeless,' he adds. 'It's part of the human condition that we like to surround ourselves with things that are a marker of something, that feel good to us but also evoke ideas.' Graham continues to ensure that his shop is one of the few places where we can do just that.

1   The Banjara are a historically nomadic trading tribe who have origins in the Mewar region of what is now Rajasthan, India. They are now found throughout northwestern, central and southern India.

2   www.anokhi.com

3   In 1971 India and Pakistan fought a battle in the Thar Desert region, which straddles the eastern border of Pakistan and the Indian western states of Gujarat and Rajasthan.

4   Parsis are an ethnoreligious group of the Indian subcontinent whose religion is Zoroastrianism. Their ancestors migrated to the region from modern-day Iran following the Muslim conquest in the 7th century CE.

5   Sindh, Baluchistan, Punjab and Khyber Pakhtunkhwa (formerly the Northwest Frontier Province).

6   The Romani, also known as the Roma, are an Indo-Aryan people, traditionally nomadic itinerants, now living mostly in Europe as well as diaspora populations in the Americas.

7   The Baluch are a group of tribes estimated at about 5 million inhabitants in the province of Baluchistan in Pakistan and also Iran and Afghanistan. The original Baluch homeland probably lay on the Iranian plateau.

8   Ann Shankar and Jenny Housego, *Bridal Durries of India*, Grantha, 1997.

9   The Vagri (Vaghri, Waghri or Baghri) are a trading caste found in Rajasthan and Gujarat in India, who handle the market in second-hand clothes. In recent times many Vagris have become prominent antique textile dealers.

10 Thames & Hudson, 2016.

Photo: Monica Fritz

above

Joss Graham in his shop in London

PIPRAU

opener
Pip Rau's collection of ikat robes
from Uzbekistan

A sensory profession

Pip Rau's life is a vivid chronicle of many of the major political events and cultural trends of the past sixty years. With her adventurous nature, artistic eye and instinct for survival, she was an early arrival in the newly established state of Israel, hung out with American beatniks in Paris and avant-garde artists in New York, was arrested and sentenced to six days in Greenwich Village Women's House of Detention for demonstrating for nuclear disarmament in Greenwich Village, travelled behind the Iron Curtain before the break-up of the Soviet Union, was one of the first to hit the hippie trail through Iran before the 1979 revolution, and formed enduring relationships in Afghanistan before and after the Russian occupation and birth of the Taliban.

Her discerning eye enabled her to seek out Central Asia's textiles and introduce their distinctive beauty to others. In the midst of it all, she raised two sons on her own, established a successful textile arts shop in London, and amassed one of the finest collections of 19th-century Uzbek ikats in the world.

Coming from a family of collectors, Rau experienced an early life that bore hints of what was to come. Her grandfather collected Louis XVI furniture, her father collected Judaica and stamps, and her mother collected little Meissen china coffee cups. Rau started her own collection of tiny glass animals when she was around ten years old. She also built up a set of little dolls in national costumes that her father would bring home for her after business trips. 'He had a really interesting life,' she says, 'travelling to South Africa, South America, Switzerland, Australia, India, the US and many other countries.' This was in the 1930s when international travel was uncommon.

The Second World War meant a four-year evacuation (1940–44) from London to Montreal when she was still a toddler, relocating with her grandmother, mother and brothers. This too presaged Rau's later experience, which saw her criss-crossing continents as a way of life. 'The boats in the Atlantic before and after us were U-boated and no one survived. We were lucky.'

Back in London she grew up in an Orthodox Jewish home with a father who thought it was important for her two brothers, but not her,

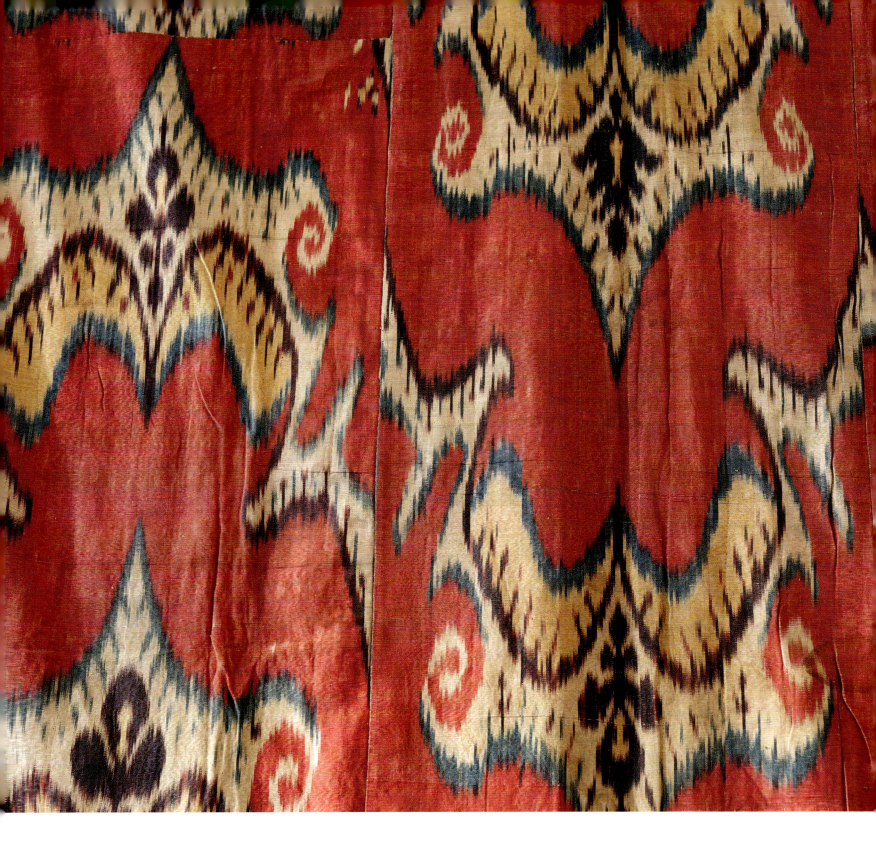

above
Detail of an Uzbek silk ikat robe from the 19th century

opposite
Souk in the Old Town of Jerusalem, 1954

All photos from Pip Rau's house: Daniel Sellam

to go to university. 'I got no encouragement so I was pretty lazy and had no aspirations,' she says of her early years. 'My brothers were actually paid to do my homework. It was easier for them to do that than to actually sit and teach me. So I never had to do much, which suited me just fine.' She was, however, 'very arty', attributing her interest to her mother, who was accomplished in that area. 'She had the eye,' Rau says. Her grandfather, who had moved to London from Germany in 1885, had already sponsored German artists who came to the English capital in the first years of the 20th century.

With academia not an option, Rau enrolled at age sixteen in Saint Martin's School of Art. It was the first of what would be a series of art schools she attended around the world over the next few years. 'Saint Martin's was exciting,' she says – but a little too exciting for her father, who soon pulled her out of school and shipped her off to her brother's kibbutz in Israel to mend her ways.

When she arrived in Jerusalem in the mid-1950s, not long after the state of Israel was established in 1948, she encountered a complex mixture of ancient and recent history. Roads were littered with burned-out vehicles left over from the struggle for statehood. Holocaust survivors bore numbers tattooed on their wrists, while the fedayeen were fighting against the Israeli government. 'I remember going to a wedding in Jerusalem, travelling in covered lorries protected by guns.'

Not keen on the physical demands of kibbutz life, in 1955 she enrolled in Bezalel, a highly regarded art school in Jerusalem. She stayed with a cousin whose father, her great-uncle Shmuel Yosef Agnon, was Israel's first Nobel Laureate for Literature (1966) By the time Rau was nineteen, both her parents had died. She decided then that 'different art schools seemed like a good way to go'. She is sure that her interest in textiles grew out of a love of art. But there would be several more art schools and tumultuous adventures before Central Asian textiles became her focus.

Back in London she re-enrolled, in 1956, at Central School of Arts and Crafts for the next two years followed by a brief stint at l'École des Beaux Arts in Paris, where she quickly tired of their 'old fashioned' approach of drawing the same pose week after week.

Interfoto / Alamy Stock Photo

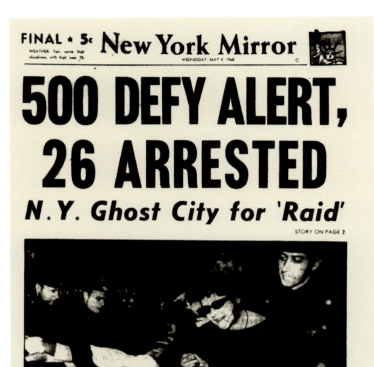

FINAL ★ 5c New York Mirror

WEATHER: Fair, some high cloudiness, with high near 78.

WEDNESDAY, MAY 4, 1960   C

500 DEFY ALERT, 26 ARRESTED

N.Y. Ghost City for 'Raid'

STORY ON PAGE 2

REFUSED TO TAKE COVER. Police bundle off two young women to the patrol wagon at City Hall. Several hundred persons refused to seek shelter and these girls were among more than a score of men and women arrested after air raid sirens warbled. (Other photos P. 2, Center Fold)

— Name It, Claim It in $2,500 Sweepstakes Game

STORY ON PAGE 5

above
Newspaper frontpage showing Pip Rau
being arrested during a nuclear
disarmament demonstration in New York,
4 May 1960

opposite top
Ikat textile

opposite bottom
Afghan kilim and pile rug

Fed up with strict academic rules, she took courses at l'Académie de la Grande Chaumière.

While neither of these Paris schools held her interest, Rau found living at the infamous Beat Hotel much more exciting. Despite its reputation as a 'flea pit' in the city's Latin Quarter, it was the chief residence in the late 1950s of American avant-garde artists and poets like Allen Ginsberg, William S. Burroughs and Gregory Corso, a crowd who gave the hotel a name that stuck and provided Rau with her first marijuana joint.

Her 'exciting' lifestyle, including living in Paris with an artist boyfriend, once again upset her family – this time a brother – who insisted she join him on a trip to the US. She fell in love with San Francisco and enrolled in the California School of Fine Arts. By 1960 she'd made her way to New York. She moved in with a boyfriend who had a Greenwich Village studio around the corner from the Cedar Bar, at the time another well-known hang-out for writers and artists like Franz Kline and Elaine and Willem de Kooning.

Commenting on her talent for often being in the right place at the right time, Rau says, 'I always felt that it was all circumstance. I had an allowance of £50 a month so I didn't have to work. I liked adventure, I liked to travel and I had nothing to keep me anywhere – I was homeless. I always had friends, friends were very important to me, and I always got by. It was all about men, like it always had been. I had fun.'

Life in New York did, at times, become serious. At a demonstration for nuclear disarmament Rau was arrested, fingerprinted, and thrown into the Greenwich Village Women's House of Detention for six days and had her photo plastered on the front page of the *New York Mirror*. 'Being in jail with murderers and prostitutes, where the guards hated us, was a real learning curve,' she says. 'That was curtains for me. I couldn't get a visa for years after that.' To this day, Rau is still sometimes taken aside at the airport and grilled by customs and immigration officers when travelling to the US to visit her son, the New York-based artist Alexander Gorlizki.

Forced back to London, she decided to go to the Soviet Union with a friend of a friend. He wanted someone with him on a drive to a conference in Yalta. Once they reached Odessa, she planned to take a boat to Israel. 'We met in Berlin and took an instant dislike to each other,' she says of her travelling companion. 'He was very right wing, I was very left.' Despite the intense animosity between them, the trip itself proved eventful in both interesting and unfortunate ways.

Starting in Berlin, they went on to Poland where she visited the Second-World-War concentration camps at Auschwitz and Birkenau, and a synagogue in Warsaw. Rau is not an observant Jew, but given her Orthodox upbringing she maintains an active interest in her Jewish heritage. The Yiddish she learned was actually from her non-Jewish

above
Strip-woven hanging with a
wool base and embroidery,
Uzbekistan, 20th century

left
Embossed and painted tin mirror,
Russia, early 20th century
opposite
Painted cupboard, Swat Valley,
Pakistan, 20th century

boyfriend in New York. Curious about the history of Jews in the places she travelled, she always looked for Jewish communities.

As they drove through the countryside in Ukraine, their car was hit by a big truck and completely destroyed. They were rescued and taken to a hospital in Uman, a nearby city with, coincidentally, a long and violent Jewish history dating back to the 18th century. During the Second World War the Germans deported the entire Jewish community, murdering thousands of them.[2]

From Uman she was moved by helicopter to the state hospital in Kirovograd, where her badly broken arm was out of commission for six weeks. From there she was flown to Odessa, met by an InTourist guide and put into a fancy hotel. One day, while out for a walk, they met a friend of the guide's who was a captain in the Soviet army. He fell in love with her. After she refused his proposal of marriage, he asked what he could do to help. Having overstayed her visa, she asked him to help get a new one and pay the hotel bill, which he did, as well as loading her up with champagne and other gifts for her boat trip from Odessa to Israel.

Rau's trip coincided with one of the few times that Russian Jews who had emigrated to Israel were permitted to return to the Soviet Union to visit their families. When they left to return to Israel, they were not allowed to take anything out of the country. By the time the boat docked in Haifa, all Rau's gifts and champagne from the captain had somehow disappeared.

Rau settled in Jerusalem in 1962 for the next nine years, where she married a well-known Israeli actor and had two babies. The youngest was born in London just before the 1967 Six Day War between Israel and its Arab neighbours including Jordan, Syria and Egypt.

Back in Jerusalem, Rau spent some of her days in markets in the diverse environment of the Old City, where her interest in textiles firmly took hold. 'That's when I first got into textiles – Palestinian dresses and shawls. Palestinian embroidery is beyond anything – it's just the most wonderful embroidery!' she says. 'I still have a great collection of the dresses and shawls which I mostly bought in 1967 or '68.'

In 1971, nine years after moving to Israel and following the break-up of her marriage, she moved back to London with her two sons. She needed to earn a living but, according to her, she was useless at everything. 'I thought I might be a driver, but I could never find my way anywhere so that was out,' she says, harking back to a time long before GPS. Rau's

cousin, the architect Heinz Rau, told her she'd never make it as an artist but she should be a buyer for a shop. 'I loved shopping and I loved travelling and I needed to make a living.' Those were the three things, she says, that motivated her to open a shop in 1974 when a friend found one for her to rent in Islington.

She flew back to Israel where she picked up various Central Asian textiles – Lakai embroideries, suzanis and ikats – from Buhkaran Jews. Many had settled there from Uzbekistan to escape the 'Black Years of Soviet Jewry', where suppression of the Jewish religion, including arrests and incarceration, had resumed after the end of the Second World War. Between 1972 and 1975, 8,000 Jews, known as 'refuseniks', managed to emigrate to Israel from the Soviet Union.[3]

From London Rau then went to Istanbul – on a package tour, because they weighed everyone's luggage as a group so she could easily bring back 100 kilos of goods. Her strategy to build up an inventory for RAU – the eponymous name of her shop – was simple: 'If I liked stuff, I bought it – textiles, jewellery, carpets, kilims, embroidery, hats, purses, decorative wood artefacts. I had no preconceived idea of what I wanted to buy.'

Some in the trade found this odd. 'Many dealers thought I was useless because I wasn't buying to make money. Money is easy come, easy go, but this stuff you can't get again. It means more. I always preferred buying to selling.' She still has some of the things she bought on that first of many buying trips to Istanbul in 1974, including a very large kilim which hangs prominently on a wall in her living room.

When she first started buying, she wouldn't spend more than £100 on anything, and she never bought antiquities because 'they could be really expensive and I had no clue what was real'. One thing she did know for sure was that she loved being surrounded by textiles, not from studying them in books but because of how they looked and felt. 'I come from a visual background, art school, travelling, markets. I've never been a studier. All my knowledge is from touching the stuff, from seeing stuff around.'

Unlike many dealers, she was not concerned with the technical aspects of textiles, relying instead on colour, beauty and whatever caught her artistic 'eye'. For her, it was 'a sensory profession'. With regard to the carpets sold in her shop, 'You learn as you deal,' she says. 'I sold loads of carpets – mostly Turkmen, Beshiri, kilims, all sorts.' Here, too, she deviates from orthodoxy, dismissing the importance of a carpet's age, how it was made and its provenance. 'You know what's good. It doesn't matter how old they are,' she says, while acknowledging that she prefers the older ones. Noting the preference among many dealers for natural dyes rather than chemicals, she insists that 'everything fades, it has nothing to do with dyes'.

opposite
Inside Pip Rau's home in Belsize Park, London
below
A collection of Christian objects
above
Turkmen silver jewellery

The shop had two floors so she sublet the upstairs to friends who already owned a store, called Hindu Kush, on the Portobello Road, on the other side of London, 'I'd barely heard of Afghanistan until then and I'd never seen things from there, but I loved what they had in their shop.' Soon she and the upstairs shop manager were engrossed in daily backgammon tournaments, ignoring whoever came in. That took its toll on their business, and Hindu Kush soon left, but it freed her up to pursue her interest in Afghanistan, since she would not be competing with her tenants.

1974 was the year Rau began her buying trips in earnest and travelled, for the first time, east of Istanbul. Driving to Afghanistan with a friend, she picked up goods along the way – embroidered blouses in Romania, carpets in Turkey, and a Qajar painting at a roadside stop in Iran. In Tehran, she discovered that most of the shops on Ferdowsi Street, the main drag she compares to Kabul's fabled Chicken Street, were owned by Jewish dealers selling antiques and textiles. After the 1979 Iranian revolution, when the country became a hard-line Islamic Republic, most of them left for places like Israel and the US.

The climax of the trip was crossing the border from Iran to Afghanistan, which she describes as magical. 'It was love at first sight. I was immediately fascinated,' she says, recalling seeing Herat for the first time. 'There were no local cars, only horse-and-cart transport, no water in the hotel, nor in the town swimming pool, and the only food available in the chai-khanas (teahouses) was big kebab, little kebab and, if you were lucky, the occasional yoghurt.'[4]

In 1976 she went to Kabul, for the first time and, from then on, her shop carried mostly things that she bought during dozens of trips to Afghanistan – often in the summer when her kids visited their father in Israel. In Kabul, a city much more Westernised than Herat, she found 'the faces of many different communities... and a great bustle and sense of excitement was everywhere. I was an Afghan junkie,' she says, appreciative of the special camaraderie among Afghans and other travellers she met there. 'Afghans have such a great sense of humour, especially the Tajiks.'

Each summer Rau would connect with a friend from Australia, a former American draft dodger whom she credits with teaching her

opposite top
Wooden carved and painted
Nandis, Rajasthan, India, early–mid-
20th century
opposite bottom
Embossed and painted tin mirror,
Russia, early 20th century

above
Carved wooden frames, Rajasthan,
India, late 19th–early 20th century

everything you need to know about carpets. 'It was a whole social scene, where everyone knew everyone, and lasting relationships were forged.' People from all over – Peace Corps workers, international dealers and local shopkeepers – would regularly gather at various shops, mostly one called Noor Sher, where lunch would be cooked for everyone.

James Opie is a well-known American carpet dealer and author, who spent years travelling to Afghanistan; he describes the lunches he attended at Noor Sher's shop:

> These lunches, with an ever-shifting assembly of guests seated on carpets, served as a gathering point for diverse figures in Noor Sher's business and social life. Dealers from several continents, an employee from a local foreign embassy, perhaps an ambassador, plus a Turkmen or Kirghiz trader fresh from smuggling merchandise across the Chinese or Soviet borders, family members, and friends all sat on the floor around large trays of rice and lamb, unleavened bread, and regional delicacies.[5]

Her extensive network of pickers, dealers and shopkeepers, established over many years, helped her locate whatever she was looking for, including most of her outstanding collection of 19th-century silk ikat textiles and coats. These pieces had rarely, if ever, been seen outside of Uzbekistan until then. 'It was art! I loved it immediately,' she says. Of all the textile arts of Central Asia, she found ikats the most exciting. The brilliance in colour and extraordinary designs reminded her of modern painting.

Though many favour the complex seven-colour ikat that comprises the renowned Guido Goldman ikat collection,[6] Rau's taste in ikat, like everything else about her, is personal. 'My favourite piece is two colours. The necessity of seven colours is bollocks.' Nor does how they're made interest her as much as the finished object. 'The look of it is what matters to me.'

top
Detail of a cushion cover, Swat Valley, Pakistan, 20th century
right
Afghan kilim
opposite
Suzani from Uzbekistan

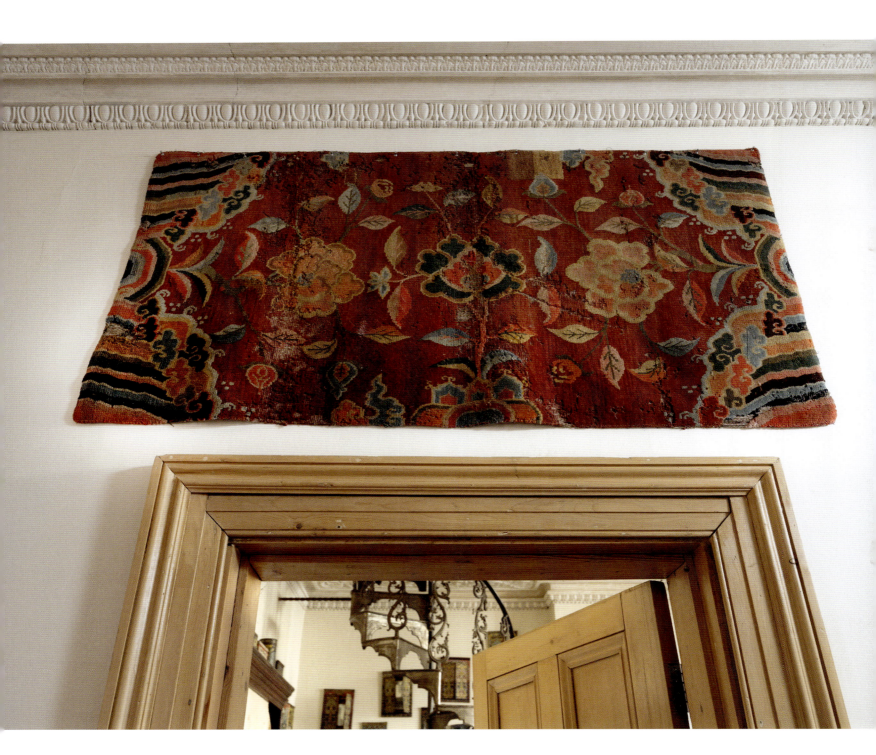

above
Tibetan khaden
opposite top
Afghan child's hat
opposite bottom
Baluch khorjin

Rau discovered that it was not possible to have a 'comprehensive' collection, since new designs had appeared for more than 100 years with guilds and workshops in several towns, each creating its own designs. There were only five or six styles for the coats, so it was the design of the ikat that created the fashion element.

She amassed most of her outstanding collection of ikat coats and textile pieces in 1978 thanks to Abdul Raouf, a Tajik dealer from Tashkurgan from whom she had previously bought a lot of different things. 'He was always good to me,' Rau says, adding that most of her Afghan colleagues were very loyal to her. When Raouf saw the newly arrived ikats, he set aside a big pile of them for her, knowing she would be interested. Meanwhile, an American dealer saw the reserved pile and was annoyed that Rau wouldn't split them with him. In retaliation, when she was about to sell these pieces to a prominent collector, the American made sure the deal was scuttled. It was a blow, she admits, but fifty-eight of those pieces are now in a museum in Taiwan.

The Soviet Union invaded Afghanistan in 1979 and occupied it for the next decade. Rau continued to travel there throughout the 1980s without any interference, but she saw and mourned the impact of the occupation on her Afghan friends.

In 1978 she ventured beyond Afghanistan to Pakistan. Her initial experience wasn't nearly as delightful as Afghanistan had been on first acquaintance. The trip from Kabul to Peshawar, a city in the western province of Khyber Pakhtunkhwa, cost a British pound and took eight hours by bus. During the Russian occupation, most of the Afghan dealers were forced to flee to Peshawar, which made Rau's subsequent trips there resemble her earlier travels as she bought mainly from the people she had got to know in Afghanistan.

From Pakistan, she headed to India. Rau's link to India goes back to 1932 when her father first travelled there. He stayed in Calcutta with members of the prominent and wealthy Sassoon family, after flights from London that, with necessary stopovers, took two weeks. Rau still has the letters he sent home.

On her first trip to India in 1975, a woman who had been to her London shop and sold her Indian clothing took her around to various shops in Delhi. Rau continued to visit the country to buy silver jewellery and some items of dress. On one of her trips to Delhi, she met a man in his shop at the Oberoi Hotel who sold books and 'really good embroideries'. Eventually, she would stay at his house on her trips and get to know the whole family, with whom she is still in touch.

Rau retained her interest in Jewish communities over the years and it led her to some interesting opportunities. Her many connections proved helpful in 1991, when a German friend that she had first met in Kabul bought an entire Torah ark and *bemah* from the Kadavumbagam Synagogue in Cochin (now Kochi).[7] Rau and her brother helped move it to The Israel Museum in Jerusalem where it was put on display along with three other reconstructed synagogues from different countries.

Rau was one of the first to assemble, promote, exhibit and publish her ikat collection as art, rather than craft, buying at source years before wealthy collectors came on the scene. Her ikat textiles were first put on display in 1986 at Abbot Hall Art Gallery in Kendal, Cumbria, followed two years later by a ground-breaking travelling show, and catalogue, at the Crafts Council Gallery in London. The exhibition travelled around the UK for two years, before arriving at galleries in Jerusalem and Baltimore. Her ikats were also exhibited in 2007 at the Victoria and Albert Museum in London, with an accompanying catalogue.

The RAU shop remained open for forty years, an impressive testament to its value for those who passed through its doors. With her characteristic modesty, Rau attributes some of its early success to an article that appeared in a British broadsheet newspaper. She was in the shop one day in late 1974 when Peter Hopkirk came in.[8] With no idea that he was a reporter for *The Times*, she started chatting with him. When they finally wrapped up some hours later he was offering to write a piece about the shop. That article, according to Rau, put the shop firmly on the map.

When the shop first opened, most of her customers associated Afghanistan solely with sheepskin coats. She sold a lot of clothing, to begin with, but her exquisite selection of textiles, jewellery, carpets, wood and decorative objects caught on. Soon her clients were 'people who just liked the stuff'. Situated next door to an Afghan restaurant, the venue was more than simply a place to do business. 'The shop did all right, but mostly it was a social thing,' Rau says. People like Steven Cohen,[9] the carpet and textile scholar, would regularly come around to reminisce about the 'good old days' in Kabul.

She held on to pieces for years, she admits, and sold them only when she needed money for her boys' school tuition. 'Last day of term I'd sell a carpet and have the cheque made out to the school.' This, she says, is because she was determined that her boys would have the good education she had been denied.

In 2004 she turned her creative spirit and painterly eye to the house she bought in 1972, creating a Gesamtkunstwerk with the many pieces she has collected over the decades. For most in the textile world, the enduring image of Pip Rau will always be one of her surrounded by jaw-droppingly beautiful Central Asian ikat textiles and silk robes, embroidered suzanis, hats and handbags, rugs and ceramics.

above
Algerian embroidered hanging and carved wooden chest and box from the Swat Valley, Pakistan
opposite
Ikat hanging, Swat Valley striped shawl, and Tashkent 'moon' suzani in the foreground

1   Saint Martin's School of Art was established in 1854, initially under the aegis of the church of St Martin-in-the-Fields. It became part of the London Institute in 1986, and in 1989 merged with the Central School of Art and Design to form Central Saint Martins College of Art and Design.

2   www.yadvashem.org/untold stories

3   https://www.jewishvirtuallibrary.org/bukharan-jews

4   Hale and Fitz Gibbon, *Ikats: Woven Silks from Central Asia: The Rau Collection*, p. 7.

5   'Find Noor Sher. Noor Sher Knows', parabola.org/2020/07/29/find-noor-sher-noor-sher-knows/

6   See Andy Hale and Kate Fitz Gibbon, pp. 144 and 166.

7   A *bemah* is a raised platform for Torah reading.

8   Peter Hopkirk, author of several books on Central Asia including *The Great Game* (1990), about the imperial struggle for supremacy there.

9   See Steven Cohen, p. 182.

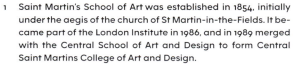

opposite
Pip Rau at home in London

above
The Torah ark and *bemah* from the
Kadavumbagam Synagogue in Cochin (now
Kochi) on display at the Israel Museum in
Jerusalem

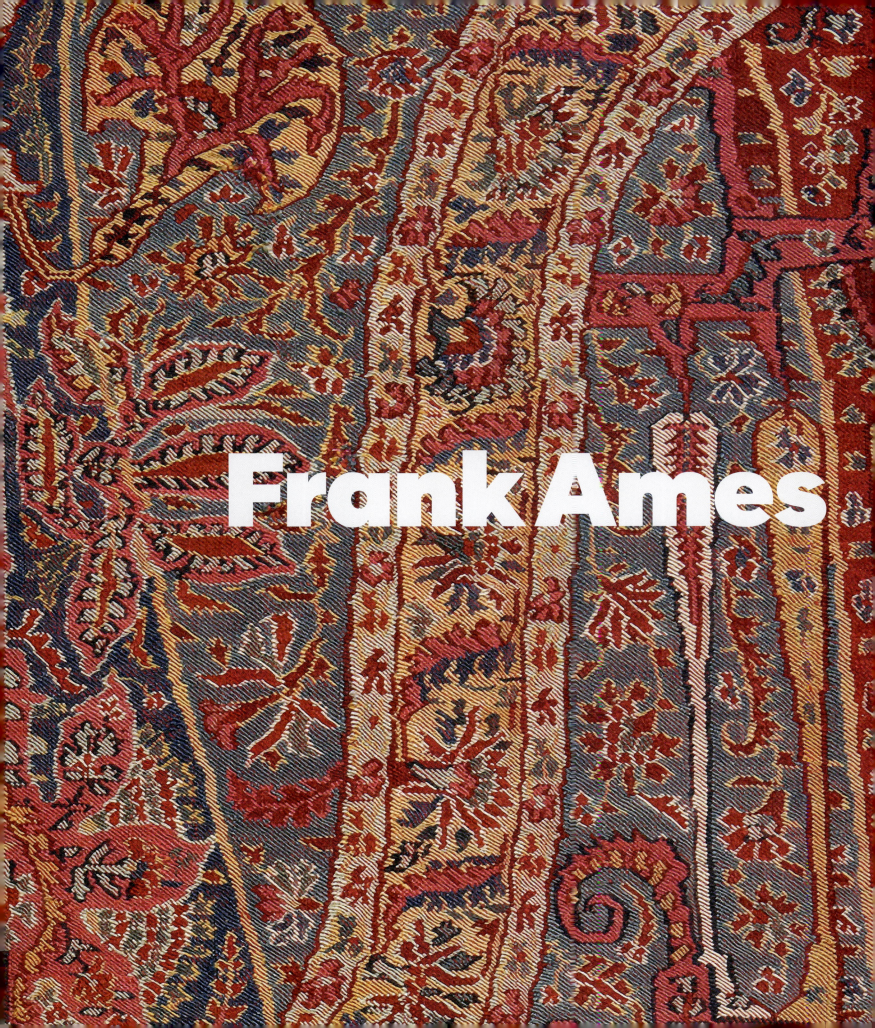

Frank Ames

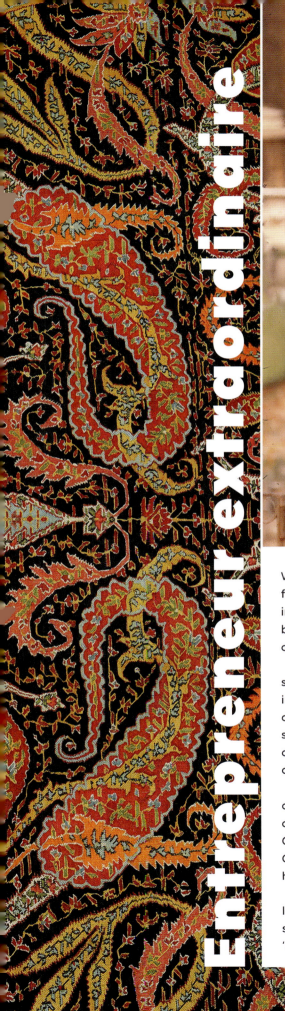

Entrepreneur extraordinaire

When the subject of Kashmir shawls comes up, Frank Ames is one of the first names to be mentioned. His two published books on the subject, involving years of painstaking original research, established him as a bona fide expert on these woven masterpieces and are a major contribution to this field of study.[1]

A tall, silent, figure, with his pierced ear, penetrating eyes and signature cotton scarf wound loosely around his neck, Ames is an intriguing character who conveys an air of mystery. His serious demeanour belies a spirited personality that, coupled with his innate street smarts, took him on an unplanned lifelong journey pursuing antiques and textiles around the world. His venturesome background is as colourful as the shawls he eventually came to be associated with.

His efforts to establish a clear historical perspective for the development of a powerful Himalayan weaving tradition have been hailed by many curators and academics. The New York Metropolitan Museum of Art, the Guimet Museum in Paris, the TAPI Collection in Surat and the David Collection in Copenhagen are just a few of the many institutions that have acquired rare, precious and unique textiles and shawls from him.

He grew up with parents who loved to see the world. Both parents loved antiques and their house was filled with them, including large, symbolist paintings from the late 19th century that hung on their walls. 'It just looked really wonderful,' he says. Although they were a Jewish

opener
Detail of a Kashmir shawl,
19th century, Khanuja
Family Collection
left
Detail of a Kashmir shawl,
19th century, Khanuja
Family Collection
above
Frank Ames
photographed on the
streets of Paris for the
*International Herald
Tribune*'s review of his first
book, *The Kashmir Shawl*,
in 1986

family (non-religious), 'We just enjoyed art for art's sake,' he says, 'no matter whether it smacked of Catholicism.' There were hints in his childhood that presaged the capricious life he would eventually lead. From the time he was six years old he was going to museums in Paris, Rome and Florence.

Ames's early life was peripatetic, moving from the upscale Upper Eastside of Manhattan to middle-class Rego Park and the idyllic enclave of Forest Hills in Queens. At one point the family were living in a twenty-eight-room mansion that was so big they only later discovered another whole family was living in one of its wings. The house came furnished with antiques of all kinds which, he remembers, they bought 'kit and caboodle'.

By the late 1960s Ames was studying electrical engineering at the NY Institute of Technology. He was hired, soon after graduation, by Grumman, an aircraft engineering company. It was the height of the Vietnam War and, rather than dodge the draft in Canada, as many of his peers were doing, he took the job. He knew engineering wasn't his calling, but it kept him out of Vietnam where, he observes, his friends were being shot. As soon as he was twenty-six, the cut-off age for the draft, he quit his job and for the next four years went to work for his dad selling used cars.

Around 1970, he bought a house in Greenwich Village, a humming New York enclave of avant-garde art, cutting-edge music and alternative culture. Each night, clubs like the Village Vanguard, Gerde's Folk City, Cafe Wha? and The Bitter End were blasting the streets with music by such musicians as Bob Dylan, Joan Baez and Charlie Mingus. Ames would play with his folk group, the Coventry Singers, at the Cafe Wha?, going on after Richie Havens and Richard Pryor.[2] The New York Studio School of Drawing, Painting and Sculpture opened in 1964 on West 8th Street, once the site of the original Whitney Museum of Art. Significant demonstrations happened in 1969 at the Stonewall Inn on Christopher Street, where a riot gave impetus to the gay liberation movement and thereby to the ongoing fight for LGBTQ rights. A safehouse in the neighbourhood for the radical anti-war movement known as the Weather Underground blew up in 1970 when an explosive device that members of the group were making accidentally detonated.

In the midst of this around-the-clock scene of activity fuelled by the creative energy of his generation, Ames fixed up his house, rented it out, took off for Europe, enrolled in Spanish classes (he was already fluent in French) and claimed that he had 'retired' at the age of 29. His inclination to live 'outside the system' was taking shape. In common with many other young Americans at this time, he didn't like US politics: Richard Nixon was in the White House, expanding the US military presence in Vietnam. Having gone to Europe and speaking French from a young age, Ames felt more European than American, and left for France with no idea of what he would do once he got there.

'My god, this is for me, this is the best,' he thought when he arrived in Paris. After settling into a rented apartment with a friend, he decided to combine the business experience he had gained with his father buying and selling cars, with the love of antiques he had cherished since childhood. Soon enough, he hooked up with an antique dealer at a Paris flea market. He tagged along with his mentor, who cruised the Paris backstreets in a taxi, popping into dozens of small antique shops in out-of-the-way pockets, selecting unusual objects that he would repair, polish and hang with a high price tag to sell to the tourists who regularly flooded the city's renowned street markets.

A major turning point came when the dealer introduced him to the famous Hôtel Drouot, where seventy independent auction firms, operating under one roof in sixteen huge, separate halls, monopolised all the auctioneering in France. 'It was a whole other world that was like Sotheby's and Christie's all rolled into one,' Ames says, and it provided the opportunity for him to strike out on his own.

During the 1970s, Drouot was still operating under France's archaic auction laws dating back to 1852. When someone died, all their possessions were put in a basket (*malette*) and brought straight to the auction sale where Ames would jostle early every morning with hundreds of rough, gruff competitors. Peering and digging through the baskets, he would hide the ones he wanted. Once home, he would pick through them and discover what items he had actually purchased – painted fans from the 18th century, 19th-century bedspreads – and decide which market would be the best one to sell each piece. He often took them to his neighbour down the road and put them on consignment with her. 'I had quite a charm with women, you know, they loved me... they couldn't wait to see what I had in the van.'

On Saturdays he would get to Drouot early, fill the van he kept in a 'box' (a term used in France for a garage) and head straight to the stand he had set up at one of the flea markets. Working as a foreigner living illegally in the country, he would have to disappear into a café across the street when the inspectors came around, waiting until they left.

above

A group of people stand outside the Cafe Wha? nightclub at 113 MacDougal Street in Greenwich Village, New York City, 21 April 1966

Since he was selling antiques, he decided that he needed to look the part. He started to dress like something out of a 19th-century novel. 'I had an earring, even then, and a full head of curly hair. I carried 19th-century antique English Gladstone bags – the kind used on stage coaches in the days of the Wild West – dressed in funky clothes and had a hat that was rakish.' Apparently people loved it.

Being 'illegal' wasn't always as easy as slipping into the closest café, and Ames had to use his wits on more than one occasion. Returning from one of his trips to Switzerland, he was questioned, in detail, by a border guard about his trips in and out of France. He thought nothing of it when he was let back into the country with no fuss. Back in Paris three days later, there was a very-early-morning pounding on his door. This was around the time when the Red Brigade in Italy and the Baader-Meinhof gang in Germany were carrying out political assassinations, robberies, arson and bombings. French-Belgian industrialist Baron Empain was kidnapped and tortured for sixty-three days in 1978. 'Tensions in Paris were high and police were carrying machine guns. There were pockets of bombings and attacks,' Ames says.

While six burly men began searching his apartment Ames, not one to scare easily, put some Brahms on the sound system and made himself some coffee. After finding some hashish on a bed table, the officers hauled him to the police station, where he had to sign documents swearing that he was not frequenting 'des bôites malfamées' (notorious clubs), and didn't have a 'box', before they let him go.

Around this time, Ames met an Australian who would shift the American's focus from a general interest in antiques to textiles, exclusively – although it would still be some time before he zeroed in on Kashmir shawls. Seeing that his friend was doing well buying and selling French antique bedcovers, Ames also started buying them at Drouot. 'I would go on Monday for the viewing, plough through all the *malettes* in each of the sixteen halls, and make detailed notes on everything I saw.'

Tuesday was the sale day, when he would aggressively compete in the rough-and-tumble auctions to buy the items he had previously noted for selection. His methodical and rigorous note-taking foreshadowed his later meticulous research on Kashmir shawls.

Every few months, he would head back to the US to visit his family. With his new interest in bedcovers, he started travelling to the antique and vintage fairs in nearby Pennsylvania buying quilts, especially the Amish ones. Being an unregistered foreigner in France meant he had to find inventive ways to avoid the unwanted attention of border guards, particularly at airports. On each trip back to Paris, he would pack ten or fifteen Italian military duffle bags and drive to the airport, where he would give a porter twenty dollars to put them on the plane, evading the

left
Auction at the Hotel Drouot, Paris
10 March 1978

risk of questions as to what he was doing with so much luggage. The cheap $99 Freddie Laker flights to Europe, and the lack of security concerns in those days, made his frequent buying trips feasible, although he would fly back to Brussels, not Paris, to minimise the risk of not being allowed back into France.

He would make trips to see friends and to shop in the antique markets on London's trendy Portobello Road, which was then a lively home to crowds of hippies with its bohemian cafés, cheap housing and happening night spots. This often involved border searches on late-night return trips that left his van dishevelled from top to bottom. At times he even had to endure a body search. Despite these 'inconveniences', his nerves of steel, preference to 'live outside the law', and natural flair for drama were assets that allowed him to live and travel where and how he wanted and to explore his growing interest in textiles.

Ames loved the antique quilts he saw in the US and Europe, and he invested much time and effort finding, selling and researching them. In preparation for an auction that he and a friend were organising in honour of the American Bicentennial in 1976, he developed his own cottage industry of women, often housewives, and many recent immigrants, to clean and repair the dirty, flea-ridden quilts. He wrote up, in French, a catalogue of the best American quilts to accompany the show. The auction was a great success. 'If you were an American in Paris back then, people liked you,' he says, attributing some of the auction success to the spirit of the time.

Inspired by the positive response, Ames dug even deeper into research about the quilts, comparing swatches at the Metropolitan Museum of Art in New York with photos he had brought from Paris of his quilts (there were only hard-copy prints back then, no digital). With the intention of writing a book about them, he travelled across the American South stopping at seniors' centres where some residents were still making quilts, drawing on memories going back to their forefathers' work on them. Despite his stalwart efforts, someone else beat him to the post, coming out with a book about the quilts before him. Disappointed, he returned to London determined to find the next 'collectible'.

Demonstrating, once again, his entrepreneurial aptitude, he quickly ruled out fields like Art Nouveau and Deco objects, areas already populated by experts who had cornered those markets, and requiring money he didn't have. Looking, instead, for something that he could afford and which would appreciate in value over time, he homed in on Kashmir shawls. 'They were relatively unknown, with little published information about them, and they were beautiful with their complex weaves, strange pashmina wool and interesting colours,' he says.

Unlike many dealers and collectors, who first fall in love with a particular kind of textile and then start to collect and sell examples,

right
Detail of a Kashmir shawl, 19th century,
Khanuja Family Collection

left
*Spinning and Weaving
Woolen Shawls, Srinagar,
Kashmir, India,* undated
photo
right
Kashmir shawl, 19th century,
Khanuja Family Collection

Ames's love affair with Kashmir shawls came after he decided to pursue them for their market potential. 'It was only after seeing the wide variety of shawl designs at flea markets and auction houses that my whole world opened up,' he says. He started buying them all around Paris and soon got 'the bright idea' to go to Paisley, Scotland, the original source of England's imitation Jacquard shawls.[3]

He would fly to Glasgow from Paris, jump into a cab which, in those days, 'was so cheap it was like taking a bus'. Relying on the driver to take him to all the antique shops in town, he would buy whatever pieces each one had while the driver waited outside, then move on to the next shop until he had done the rounds. From there they drove to Paisley, twenty minutes away, where he met the present-day members of weaving families that went back to the 19th century. 'Before you knew it I had twenty to thirty pieces. Then I'd get on the train to Edinburgh, do the same thing there and take a late flight home with about fifty pieces.'

After several trips back and forth he had accumulated a couple of hundred 19th-century shawls which were stacked up in his apartment. Now came the eureka moment when, Ames says, his learning curve shot way up as he began to sort and study them, and prepare them for auction. 'You get the feel for which pieces are English and which French – the

above
Frank Ames at his first Kashmir shawl
auction at Drouot in Paris, circa 1974
right
Detail of a Kashmir shawl, 19th century,
Khanuja Family Collection

colours, the quality of the weave, the quality of the wool, the fringing.' Writing a catalogue for them was a challenge, he says, 'because I had to describe pattern and design when there was a bare minimum of information available aside from a lone book by John Irwin of the V&A, and a small catalogue from a 1975 exhibit at Yale University'.

In addition to the buying and sorting, and researching and writing the catalogue, Ames also did the promotion for the auction by hanging posters in cafés and plastering them on walls all over Paris; it was old-fashioned foot work to get the word out, he notes.

With the arrival of books devoted to specific categories of antiques, auctioneers began to specialise. Instead of auctioning lots of mixed antiques – furniture, paintings, textiles, jewellery – in one sale, they were starting to streamline the sales into discrete categories. It was a new way of doing business and change was in the air after decades of conformity. Ames's timing was just right. The auction was a huge success. 'Two hundred Kashmir shawls hanging on a wall – nobody ever saw that before. Everything sold!'

The auction brought in people from all walks of life along with all the top designers in Paris from haute couture. 'It was amazing to watch all these very sophisticated people leaving the auction sale with all this stuff under their arms.'

After the triumph of the auction, Ames was inspired to continue with the shawls. He started to carefully organise his research on them. 'Every time I went to a museum or a library, like the Bibliothèque Nationale in Paris, to study their collection, I'd make notes on index cards.' He would meet with curators hoping to learn more, but was surprised to discover that most knew nothing about what they had in their collections and no one was studying them or giving them serious interest.

When confronted with this lack of information, Ames decided to do what had worked for him before – go directly to the source, in this case India and Kashmir. He sold his place in Greenwich Village, as luck would have it, to a Rockefeller Foundation official who obligingly wrote introductory letters for him to major museums in India.[4]

By now it was 1979 and Ames was excited and ready to begin his fieldwork on Kashmir shawls. 'So here I am, I'm gung-ho, I've got my cameras, I've got my film – I got off the plane in Delhi ready to kill.' Instead of what he hoped for, however, he soon discovered that the opportunities for research were not much better there than in Europe.

When he went to the National Museum in Delhi and met the director, he was faced with a brick wall of bureaucracy 'Sorry, but the collection can't be seen until two weeks from now,' he was told; and on it went, one bureaucratic roadblock after another. The museum in Benares yielded better results, even though, for no apparent reason, he was told he could only shoot photos in black-and-white. Not one to simply follow orders, he changed the labels from colour to black-and-white on his film canisters, and shot thousands of colour photos – sometimes

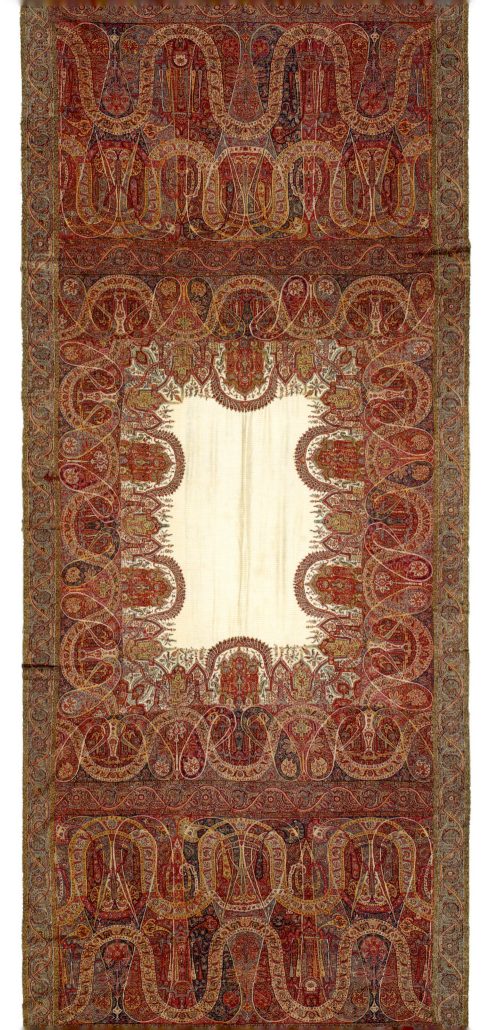

Kashmir shawl and detail,
High Sikh Period, circa 1835,
Khanuja Family Collection

thirty or forty shots of the same shawl just to make sure he captured it – of their impressive collection.

At this point, the idea of writing a book on the shawls hadn't yet crystallised. 'I was just doing it out of interest,' he says, recalling how he enjoyed meeting dealers and seeing great textiles. This two-month trip was the first of many he would make to India and Kashmir, at least once or twice every year, after he realised that he would have to be the one to write a book about the shawls given that no one else was interested.

Over his many visits, Ames left no stone unturned in observing and trying to understand all aspects of the shawl-making process. He put an ad in *Kitab*, Srinagar's local paper, asking anyone who had old photos, fragments or other documentation to contact him. He spent hours and hours with dealers looking through their stocks, hanging out with them, and buying pieces. He visited Najibabad, about 200 kilometres north of Delhi, where many people remain devoted to repairing old shawls.

He sat down with the weavers in Kashmir to learn how to do it – to get a feel for it – which would be impossible now, owing to the political conflict there. Even then there was risk. 'One of my best friends was shot in the arm driving his brother to the airport. Indian officers just opened fire,' he recalls. All the right conditions for making the shawls existed in Kashmir, Ames concluded, thanks to its high-quality wool and 2,000 years of perfecting the dyeing technique using the 'magical' qualities of water from the Jhelum River.

Back in Paris, he would project shawl designs onto a white sheet and, using a 2HB pencil, trace them, turn the projector off and closely examine the drawings. 'You don't really see much on a slide or in a book. I wanted to see them up big.' Ames got the idea to blow up the images from studying French art history and noting how painters of the past copied the shawls meticulously. 'Ingres and other artists from the Napoleonic era draped personages in shawls that they painted quite authentically. He discovered old publications from the 1830s with traced shawls, which validated their existence at that time. In his second book, the photos are blown up to best reveal the details.

Ames had been doing all the research, travel and studying the shawls on his own until 1981, when he secured a publisher and an advance of $5,000. Then the oil crisis hit and he was told that there weren't enough pre-orders to go ahead with publication.[5] Although he was disappointed, in the end it turned out to be a good thing when he realised the book wasn't up to the standard he was aiming for. After he worked on it for another whole year, a prestigious niche publisher released *The Kashmir Shawl and Its Indo-French Influence* in 1986.

Because so little had previously been written about Kashmir shawls, Ames had to find effective, creative ways to approach the subject and develop a vocabulary to write about it. His eclectic

left
Detail of a Kashmir shawl, 19th century,
Khanuja Family Collection
above
Frank Ames at the Red Fort in Agra,
India, circa 1981

method included careful study of a related subject in which he had already developed an interest in Paris. 'If you really want to study a textile it's good to have a contrasting perspective from a peripheral related textile.' For him, it was antique carpets, as well as Mughal history and Mughal art which, he says 'takes you all the way down the brick road'. Even though his second book focuses on the Sikh period, there's a whole chapter on the Mughal period, to give it narrative continuity. He also studied poetry. 'I wanted to know if any Persian poets talked about textiles, or if Kashmiri poets talked about the weaving of shawls, because they were such an important part of daily life.'

Ames regards his classification of the Indian shawls into Mughal, Afghan, Sikh and Dogra periods as best representing his contribution to the field. But he asserts that his greatest achievement is his discovery of a new form of Indian art: the mysterious Sikh patterns that evolved under Maharaja Ranjit Singh (1780–1839). He acknowledges that many other subjects he touched in his research could also provide fertile ground for others. 'I couldn't spend another six or seven years on another book. My last book just took the wind out of me.'

After his years of fieldwork and research on the shawls, he was especially gratified that the results were well received in India, and elsewhere. At the same time his theories have been met with some resistance, primarily from certain academics who, he believes, don't understand his proposal that the Sikh patterns came from the 'soil of the Punjab', not Europe.

His enthusiasm and commitment remain undimmed. As he states on his website, 'In all my years of dealing in India's diverse textiles ... I've found no other capable of taking the breath away as dramatically as the scintillating richness of a super fine Kashmir shawl spread out before the eyes to behold. These are the true bijoux of the Himalayas.'

1   Frank Ames. *The Kashmir Shawl and Its Indo-French Influence.* Antique Collectors Club, January 1986; *Woven Masterpieces of Sikh Heritage: The Stylistic Development of the Kashmir Shawl under Maharaja Runjit Singh, 1780–1839.* ACC Art Books, June 2010.

2   Ames' folk group, 'The Coventry Singers', performed regularly during the 1960s at the Café Wha and Bitter End.

3   By the 1820s, so many Paisley shawls were being churned out that the town's name became synonymous with the patterns, which of course derived in part from the Indian shawls hand-woven in Kashmir. Trading brought them to Europe in the late 18th century, and soon after 1800 similar shawls were being made first in Norwich and Edinburgh and then Paisley.

4   The Rockefeller Foundation was set up in 1913 to 'promote the well-being' of humanity. Its scope includes medical, scientific, agricultural and artistic enterprises as well as international relations.

5   Reduced demand for oil in the 1980s, coupled with increased production, resulted in a dramatic decline in prices and damage to world economies.

above
Frank Ames surrounded by textiles at the Triple Pier Antiques Show in New York City, 1988

Elizabeth Hewitt

When Elizabeth Hewitt began collecting hair dryers in high school, no one imagined she would end up years later in a place remote to most Westerners, producing textiles for one of the world's most celebrated fashion designers. In what sounds like the plot of a Cold War spy story, she would hunt down the only two living *ustas* (masters) in Uzbekistan with the knowledge and skills to weave traditional 19th-century ikat designs, surmount the myriad bureaucratic obstacles in the former Soviet Republic, and smuggle the finished fabric out of the country for fashion guru Oscar de la Renta.

Hewitt's audacious journey from hair dryers to haute couture and beyond began in her grandmother's attic in Pittsburgh. Every time she went to her house, they would go through boxes and boxes of quilts from her great grandmother and great-great grandmother. 'She would call herself a "junker" but my grandmother was an antique collector,' says Hewitt. 'She had a great eye and tons of textiles and embroideries.' Grandmother would buy handmade blankets for a dollar from the Amish, who lived nearby. Years later, when Hewitt showed one to a dealer, he said it was worth at least a few thousand dollars. But she was unable to part with it; the blanket is stored, along with the vintage hair dryers, in her mother's basement.

Oh, this is going to be my job!

Given her background, it might seem obvious that Hewitt would become a textile collector, dealer and designer, but it took a while, and the influence of an important mentor, before she realised it was what she wanted to do. After graduating from high school in 1987, she enrolled in a general arts programme, taking mainly art classes at the University of Connecticut. Her parents, however, weren't keen on her future as an artist and neither did she feel that she was good enough to make a life of it. She decided, instead, to become an interior designer and transferred to the Philadelphia College of Textiles and Science[1] where one of her first classes was textile design. 'I'd never heard of it before. I thought, oh my god, I could paint and have a job!' It was in that class that she realised, for the first time, that she had always loved textiles.

The college was an industry school. Students from all over the world, many of whose parents owned textile factories, came to learn the trade in order to eventually take over the family business or work at one of the big textile manufacturing companies. In her senior year Hewitt took a weaving class with Bhakti Ziek,[2] who ran the woven design course. Ziek, an artist and a weaver who had studied textiles and backstrap weaving in Mexico and Guatemala, was a major early influence. She encouraged Hewitt's development as a textile artist, rather than a commercial designer, when her other professors were calling her colourways odd and her work unsaleable.

'Bhakti was super cool and she really liked me. All of the projects I did for her were art, not weaving.' Hewitt also credits Ziek with introducing her to the books and work of textile pioneer Jack Lenor Larsen,[3] who became another important influence and inspiration. Years later, with her future husband (who had a carpet shop), she had the pleasure of playing host to Larsen in Istanbul and Konya. 'We looked at embroideries, felts and all kinds of textiles,' she says. She showed him some Japanese Meisen textiles she had just brought back from Burma and he explained how they used 'weft markers' to make them. Two of her own designs are inspired by exactly those fabrics.

The school prided itself on its high job-placement record in the commercial textile industry. Hewitt was the exception. They would call and berate her, after she graduated, for ruining their statistics, urging her to go to work for the industry. 'That was never going to happen with my portfolio full of dogs in Victorian windows, alligators with a hair dryer, and odd-coloured striped prints.'

Hewitt's hunt for global textiles began during her summer breaks when she travelled to Morocco and India, always on the lookout for handmade objects, mainly textiles. After she graduated, she spent six months in Ecuador where she bought some 'exquisite' blue-and-white ikat shawls with lace ends that, she says, you can no longer find. 'I bought a bunch of them and when I came back to Philadelphia someone with a little textile shop offered me what seemed like a lot of money for them.' This was a turning point when she realised 'Oh, this is going to be my job!' Then the 'hunting and gathering' began in earnest.

In Turkey in 1994 she saw a guy open up his shop and shake out a suzani, an embroidered textile from Uzbekistan, that she had never seen before. Uzbekistan, one of the former Soviet republics in Central Asia, was starting to open up its borders to Western travellers just a few years after the break-up of the Soviet Union in 1991. Uzbeks had been creating suzanis, and other handmade goods, all through the Soviet era, but only for themselves or to sell elsewhere in the Soviet Union. After communist control arrived in the 1920s, nothing could be exported to the West.

Through dogged perseverance and a little good luck, Hewitt was there at the beginning of the flood of textiles pouring into Turkey from Uzbekistan and other Central Asian countries. She had met an Afghan dealer living in the US who told her to go to where the Uzbeks were in Istanbul instead of buying from the dealers in the bazaar. After much cajoling, he took her to the dirty, dusty depots where everything was being dumped.

The Afghan-born Uzbeks in Turkey were first on the scene when Uzbekistan was just starting to open up. Originally dealers in Afghanistan, they were forced to flee from war at home to Pakistan and, after encountering more difficulties there as refugees, they moved to Turkey.

Hewitt had flown to Pakistan a few times in 1994 and 1995 to buy textiles – Lakai, Kungrat, kilims, small embroideries – and jewellery, but it was difficult. 'Peshawar was definitely a man's world,' she says, noting the

opposite
Saydona hand-tied, dyed and woven ikat fabric, Tulu Textiles. Original design by Elizabeth Hewitt

above
Woman with silkworm cocoons
in Uzbekistan
opposite
Man wrapping warp for ikat
dyeing in Uzbekistan

difference between her experience there and other male dealers who loved the place. On her second trip to the city she had stayed with an Afghan family who insisted she sleep in the only bed (which was like an army cot) with the grandmother. The rest of the family slept on cushions on the floor. 'Not a great night's sleep,' she says, 'but it was a lot of fun.' She eventually came to the conclusion that Istanbul had much more available to buy and was more pleasant, especially for a single young woman.

Soon Hewitt was seeing Afghan dealers she had met in Peshawar in Istanbul. These roving merchants gradually established an Afghan Street in the Grand Bazaar reminiscent of Kabul's famed Chicken Street, with crowded little shops overflowing with textiles and carpets.

In 1995, she flew to Uzbekistan where she discovered that, even though the country was starting to open up, ordinary Uzbeks were struggling. She paints a bleak picture in which there were no vegetables and people had no money. 'The big bazaar in Tashkent was completely empty. There was no tourism so they had to go to Turkey and sell their personal possessions.' That's why in the 1990s there were more suzanis

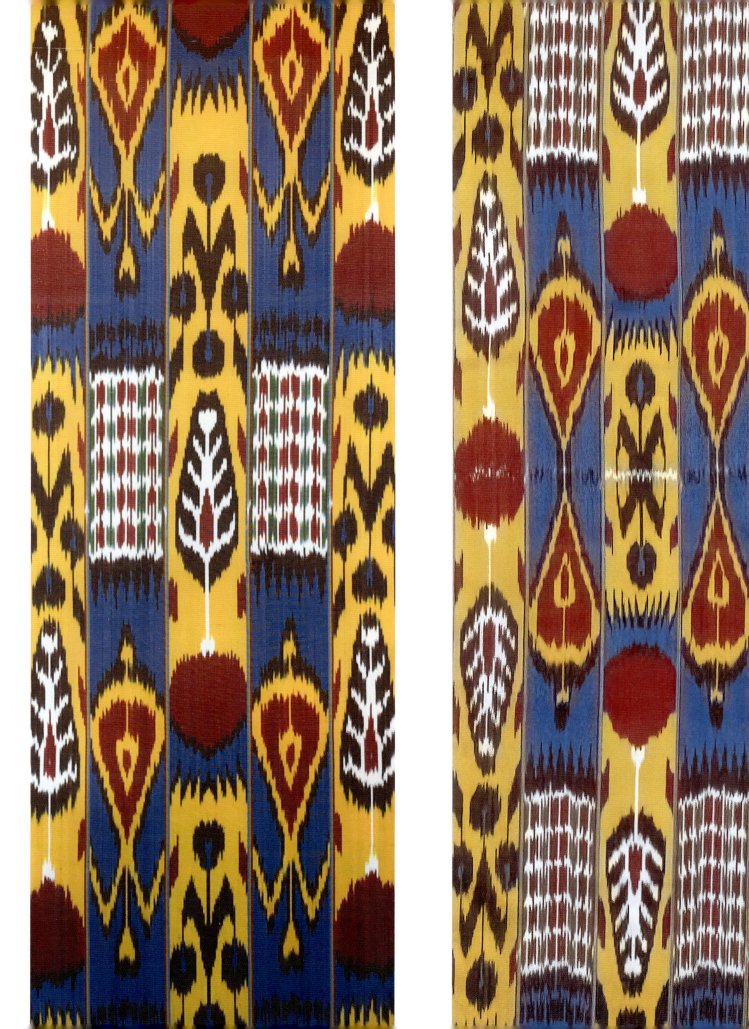

and other Uzbek textiles in Istanbul than Uzbekistan. While there may not have been many tangible results from her first trips to the former Soviet republic, Hewitt's instinct to get an early understanding of the country paid off later, when she introduced ikat, made using traditional 19th-century production techniques, to the West.

Since it was difficult to export goods out of Uzbekistan, Hewitt relied on an unofficial network of women whom she calls 'the ladies'. They would manoeuvre their way through customs to deliver goods to Turkey. 'The ladies have their own methods,' Hewitt says. 'They're traders – they come and go. In Istanbul they buy gold, take it back and sell it in Uzbekistan.' There in the dingy Istanbul depots, far from the splendid halls of the popular Grand Bazaar, they would unload 'stacks and stacks of amazing material' where the 'dealers to the dealers to the dealers' would have their pick.

'In a day I would buy hundreds of antique Lakai embroideries, Kungrat and Turkmen textiles, tassles and suzanis galore, for zero money.' She was seeing an extraordinary number of carpets and textiles and getting a first-hand education about them that no classroom anywhere could offer. 'It was like getting a master's degree,' she says.

Meeting an Afghan Uzbek family in Istanbul was fortuitous for Hewitt in more ways than one. Besides introducing her to the Uzbek dealers in the Istanbul depots, where she would do most of her buying, the family also had a house in Uzbekistan where she stayed on some of her early buying trips. The family took her to villages where she met the women and saw the way they used suzanis in their homes, where male dealers weren't allowed to go.

It was illegal to stay in a private house at that time. You had to have an official stamped hotel receipt for every night you stayed to show at customs when you were leaving the country. Her hosts would take her passport and pay a 'little extra' to get a hotel stamp. Other times, she stayed in the old 'official' Soviet tourist hotels which were rundown and expensive. They used the exorbitant official exchange rate instead of the much lower black-market rate. Young girls lounging around the lobby were available for the night or by the hour.

In 1993 she started selling in the US what she was buying abroad, going to stores and galleries with her wares. By 1995 she had begun setting up a booth at ethnographic shows, like the Tribal Art Show in San Francisco and the Los Angeles Gift Show, but it would be some years before she could devote herself entirely to textiles. She would earn enough to travel, see and buy as many textiles as possible. 'I would go on big three-month trips, come back, sell, waitress, bartend, and do a show,' she says, describing a demanding routine that lasted seven years. It wasn't until 2000 that she could quit her last bar-tending and waitressing jobs.

At this point she was living in San Francisco with four roommates in a 'big old ugly house' where she couldn't invite 'someone fancy', so she would make appointments to visit other dealers and galleries. 'Textiles were so hot,' she says. 'It was a sort of heyday from the mid-nineties to the early 2000s for ikat, suzanis and all kinds of Central Asian materials. There were plenty of collectors – people who had travelled a bit and had money.'

A great deal was happening to introduce and promote these relatively unknown materials. The de Young Museum was expanding its collection. The book on Guido Goldman's ikat collection[4] was published during this time and the collection, at Goldman's insistence, was being exhibited only at fine art museums instead of the more usual tribal and craft galleries, providing exposure to a whole new class of potential buyers.

Top dealers, like the late Michael Andrews in Marin County, San Francisco, would call Hewitt insisting that she call him first when she arrived back from Turkey with a new shipment. 'I would go to his house and show him everything. He would buy a ton of stuff, always telling me I had to charge more,' she says, referring to him as another mentor. Other California clients included James Blackmon, another top dealer for goods from Central Asia. In 1995 she met textile collector Fred Krieger, who was active in ACOR (the American Conference of Oriental Rugs). He and his wife Stella introduced her to other collectors and invited her to stay in their home in Los Angeles when she was there for the fairs. 'Fred was really important for my growth as a dealer,' she says. 'Fred, Stella and I became fine friends, and they were very generous – always connecting me with people.'

Most of the dealers at that time were from the generation that had travelled to Afghanistan, Pakistan and India in the 1970s, or were well-established Turkish dealers. They had gained knowledge about the value of the textiles they were selling and had built up some financial resources. Hewitt, who was one of the first to tap into the newly available antique Uzbek textiles flowing into Turkey, was much younger and had fewer financial resources than most of them. This, she believes, put her at a disadvantage. At the northeastern Black Sea port of Trabzon, established Turkish dealers

opposite
Ikat fabric in a traditional style produced
by Elizabeth Hewitt and her team of
weavers and dyers in Uzbekistan

would wait for boats loaded with trash bags full of textiles from Central Asia. 'They would hand over $500 per bag without even opening them,' Hewitt says. Some of these sacks were full of 19th-century ikat coats. Smart dealers would buy bags and bags and wait to sell the rare pieces they contained as their value increased over time. 'I couldn't afford to do that, but I would pick for myself some of the things I loved, like Lakai embroideries,' she says. 'Then I would get to a point where I needed money and would have to sell them. At fairs, I always did more business selling to the more established dealers during the days of set-up than at the fair itself.'

Because she was a young, relatively new female dealer, certain people didn't want to spend a lot of money with 'some random, travelling girl'. One time, she recalls, such an attitude backfired when a couple who were eyeing up some Kyrgyz and Kungrat embroideries decided she wasn't 'at their level'. When they returned some time later, having changed their minds, the embroideries had all been sold to a knowledgeable collector who knew quality when he saw it and didn't mind who was selling it.

At one tribal art fair in San Francisco she was pleased when she sold for $900 one of the three Tashkent suzanis she had bought for $300 each. Unbeknown to her, a more established dealer had a similar single suzani for sale in his booth for $18,000. He had probably bought his suzani in the 1980s, Hewitt says, when it was believed that only a few pieces like it existed and could fetch such large sums. After 1991, when suzanis of even better quality flooded the market, the price fell dramatically.

'Do you have some old ikat pieces?' Oscar de la Renta asked Elizabeth Hewitt some time in 1999. One of his assistants had met her at a tribal art fair and invited her to show some textiles to the famous fashion designer for inspiration. So, 'I would schlep over some antique textiles a couple of times a year when I was in New York,' she says.

In 2001 Hewitt attended a show in Milan with fellow Istanbul dealer Seref Ozen where they realised that some of the velvet ikat that looked antique was actually new. It occurred to them that some of what was being sold as 19th-century ikat in Istanbul, at a very high price, was entirely new. No one had grasped the fact that such high quality was still being produced, which is why they had all assumed it was antique.

Ozen was good at spotting the contemporary pieces being sold in Istanbul. They started trying to find out who made them. That led them to two Afghan-Uzbek brothers living in Istanbul who were importing ikat from Uzbekistan. Hewitt began buying from them and selling their ikat to American interior designers. They asked for more of the same designs and colours they had bought but, despite the brothers agreeing to fulfil the orders, the ikat either never came or something completely different would arrive.

Hewitt flew to Tashkent in 2004 to investigate the problem. Nimetullah, one of the brothers, took her to a big empty building where an Uzbek named Bakijon and his daughter were weaving on a couple of looms. Bakijon had been brought to Tashkent from the Fergana Valley, where the dyers and weavers were, to prevent Hewitt from meeting them all. She ordered 200 metres of four ikat designs on that trip. After days of negotiation, they agreed to provide it.

On her next visit to the Oscar de la Renta offices, that year in August, she showed the ikat samples to the head textile designer, who was so excited she brought Oscar in to see them. When he saw the samples, he changed his catwalk show, scheduled for the next month, to include the ikat. 'I couldn't have imagined when I walked in that day with the samples that Oscar was going to immediately put it on the runway,' Hewitt says.

That afternoon Hewitt was called back to the ODLR offices and, after getting caught in a sudden downpour, she arrived at one of the world's most elegant fashion houses 'looking like a drowned rat in baggy Levi jeans and a soaking-wet little linen top'. As she had never worked in fashion before, they had to explain the whole process to her, from the runway to retail and everything in between. They told her they would order 500 metres if the designs succeeded on the runway; if that sold well, they would place a second and maybe a third order. 'I thought sure, we can do that,' she says.

The first six models in the runway show walked out wearing ikat. The ikat trench coat was prominently displayed on the front page of the *Wall Street Journal International* and was featured, years later, in an exhibition at the George Washington University Textile Museum in Washington, DC.[5] One of the pieces was an extremely complicated seven-colour ikat design. Nobody today could make it, says Hewitt, but back then she thought she had found the master who could.

A few days after the show Hewitt got a fax from the ODLR offices with an order for 5,000 metres instead of the 500 metres they had previously told her. ODLR hadn't considered the particularly narrow width of ikat, and that in combination with the show being such a high seller meant that they actually needed the greater length. Soon the reality hit of what she had committed to. 'I nearly died from stress and anxiety,' she says. She feared, based on her previous experience, that the brothers couldn't provide a consistent large quantity of the high-quality ikat designs – with just the right weight of the silk and density of the warp – that she had signed a contract to deliver.

'I was calling and calling Nimetulleh. When he finally brought me a bag of ikat in Istanbul it didn't look anything like what I had shown Oscar. He insisted it was the same, but it wasn't.' She hopped on a plane to Uzbekistan, climbed into a tiny car with four local men and started

above

Ikat fabric in a traditional style produced by Elizabeth Hewitt and her team of weavers and dyers in Uzbekistan

opposite

A model wears an ikat coat by Oscar de la Renta at Fashion Week in New York, September 2004. The fabric was produced by Elizabeth Hewitt and her team in Uzbekistan

driving around to find out what was going on. 'Every single ikat was wrong – wrong colour, terrible quality.' Unbeknown to her, Bakijon, the master weaver, had fought with the brothers, walked out, and refused to make anything more for them.

She was getting calls from Oscar's office on her old Nokia phone asking where everything was. 'I was driving around villages in the middle of the night checking looms and warps – everything was wrong but I was saying to them, yes, yes, sending some fabric soon, when I actually didn't have even one metre.' By now, Hewitt had found out about Bakijon's exit. He was the only one who could make the most complex of the four sample designs that used seven different colours. She was desperate to find him.

Word about the success of the show had appeared in the Uzbeki press. Everyone was proud of it and the hotel waiters, receptionists and others were bombarding Hewitt with pictures of their ikat and volunteering their 'cousins' as *ustas*. She tried other *ustas* but no one even came close to Bakijon. 'It was a miracle,' she says, when Nimetullah's estranged nephew contacted her and told her where to find Bakijon. 'Take me to him,' she said, not believing him after all the 'cousins' that had been proposed. When she actually found Bakijon in the city of Namangan, in the Fergana Valley, she had to work secretly with him since he and the brothers weren't speaking.

The second order for another 5,000 metres came before the first 5,000-metre order was completed; and another, smaller order came in January. 'Everything was delivered late, but there was no other way for them to get the fabric so they had to wait,' Hewitt says, listing one problem after another that she had to face. Sometimes the fabric would be stained, or she couldn't get the same dye bath each time because they couldn't always obtain the Chinese dyes, which are better than the Russian ones; or the dyers would try to cut corners and use the Russian dyes; or they had to bring red from Turkey. In the beginning, the dyers never wrote down their recipes, as this kind of sustained 'production' was new to them. In the winter, when it was freezing cold and dark, there was often only enough electricity for a couple of hours a day. Islam Karimov, the country's post-Soviet President (1989–2016), wouldn't send natural gas because political dissidents were in the Fergana Valley. Hewitt brought battery-powered lanterns from Turkey for the weavers, which helped a little. But a couple of times her visa applications were denied.

She was there for months, checking every day and through the night, during Ramadan, living in a dirty, bug-infested hotel to ensure that everything was being done right. When she reported a rat in her room, the receptionist smiled, opened a drawer, and pointed to a gun.

The logistics giant UPS eventually opened up in Uzbekistan, but shipping with them didn't work out because you couldn't bring out more than four metres of anything, old or new. Hewitt had to continue shipping underground using 'the ladies'. Each time 200 metres were ready Hewitt would have the 'ladies' take it to Turkey, where it had to be washed. Karimov's dictatorship didn't want anyone to make a living from private enterprise. 'We had to set up a washhouse in Konya and learn how to deal with thousands of metres of fabric before it was sent to New York.' That was something totally new for her. 'I felt the whole time that we could never do it, never manage, and that I would be sued and it would be a disaster.'

After the success of that first show, Hewitt started creating new designs in December 2004 for the autumn 2005 runway; she knew that, if there was any chance of selling ikat to Oscar again, it would have to be a totally different look with new designs. This time she made velvet and thick satin ikat in wide horizontal stripes. Even though she was working with Bakijon, it was hard to teach the masters how to use traditional techniques while making something that was not a traditional design. 'They had never done anything like that before so there was a big learning curve,' she says. She even had to consult her old teacher Bhakti Ziek, an expert weaver, about the proper density of the warps to achieve 19th-century-quality ikat. The dye for one of the velvet batches didn't set properly and had to be dry cleaned seven times in Turkey before it was fixed. 'When the models wore the dress on the runway, they turned green! I got a very angry phone call the next day,' she says.

Some of the satins in the autumn 2005 show were made at Yodgorlik, the government-run silk factory in the Fergana Valley city of Margilan, but Hewitt preferred to work with the independent masters where the quality was superior and conditions were better for the workers with children. 'I had weavers and dyers working in their homes. No one had to leave home to go to work, and they could work on their own time.'

When Oscar de la Renta's models strutted down the catwalk wearing the little-known textile, ikat designs took off. 'Oscar really started the ikat explosion,' says Hewitt. She continued to design and produce original ikat fabric for each of Oscar's four yearly runway shows through to 2010, watching as the national textile of

Uzbekistan began turning up on fashion front pages and in wardrobes and interiors around the world. Designer Donna Karan did two seasons using ikat, and others in the fashion world were eager to follow. Interior designer Michael Smith used Hewitt's ikat textiles in the home of celebrity fashion model Cindy Crawford, which was featured in *Elle Decor* magazine.

Hewitt was also selling to renowned London interior designer Robert Kime. He had been collecting antique ikat for years when Hewitt first met him in Istanbul and was one of the first to use ikat textiles on upholstery. With the high cost of antique ikat, and the supply running out, Hewitt started producing thousands of metres of high-quality, handmade ikat. And even back in 2005 she was supplying ikat textiles to New York designer Madeline Weinrib, who was selling it from her Manhattan studio on the top floor of the ABC Carpet & Home store. Hewitt continued to produce ikat for Weinrib until she closed her studio in 2019, by which time her unique ikat design and colour adaptations were world famous.

Hewitt had always wanted to live in Istanbul and, when she realised there was nothing holding her back, she moved there in 2003. 'I always thought India would be the place for me – I love everything about India,' she says, 'but Istanbul is home. I really feel good there, even with all its problems.'

By 2008 Hewitt was married to Hüseyin Kaplan, a carpet dealer from Konya, and pregnant with their daughter, while Kaplan's brother, Muzaffer, was looking for a new place for his shop in Istanbul. When he found an old house with room to spare, Hewitt suggested they open a retail shop. 'Istanbul was bumping in those days,' she says, 'so we just did it!' She describes Muzaffer as a 'dealer's dealer with a great eye'.

She had already started block printing a line of bedding and fabric in India, and was well into making ikat in Uzbekistan. She had been travelling back and forth to India and Indonesia where she saw interesting furniture, beaded baskets and other beautiful items. 'I wanted to make the store a home store, because in Istanbul you had to hunt forever to buy an antique Turkish table. There was only Ikea, ugly 1970s Turkish furniture, or expensive high-end design from Italy.'

When she first started dealing in the 1990s, she was buying everything – carpets, kilims, tulus and textiles as well as jewellery. At one show, she had an entire booth of old tulu carpets,[6] so it wasn't surprising when she called the new shop Tulu, which also happened to be her dog's name. Located on a quiet street in the charming old neighbourhood of Sultanahmet, the store garnered international acclaim, landing on the Condé Nast list of hot spots in Istanbul and earning numerous write-ups in *Elle Decor*, *House Beautiful*, *Maison Française* and many other leading interiors publications. *One Kings Lane* called it a 'fabric fantasyland': 'In a lovely old townhouse, this four-story showroom is filled with American expat Elizabeth Hewitt's gorgeous hand-blocked linens, coveted by stylists, designers, and celebrities the world over.'

In 2017 Tulu scaled down to two floors from four, and became a 'by appointment' operation in Istanbul, with a website that takes orders.[7] And in 2019 Hewitt and Kaplan joined forces with long-time friend and textile designer Clare Louise Frost to open Tamam,[8] a mini version of Tulu, in New York's trendy East Village.

Hewitt may not have ended up at a big commercial textile manufacturing company as her teachers had wished, but her years studying textile design did not go to waste. Her first attempt at designing modern carpets – in 2002, along with a partner – did not, however, achieve commercial success. 'Our carpets were so beautiful but, with the cost of production higher in Turkey than Nepal, nobody cared because of the price.' Unable to compete in the market for this reason, they closed the carpet design business in 2007. By then Hewitt had already successfully pioneered traditional ikat production in Uzbekistan.

Meanwhile, she also took an interest in Indian block printing to expand her reach. She was craving drawing and printing, and wanted to be able to print those images. She began to work with a family in Jaipur who still produce her designs today because 'they know how to create the look I want', she says. In India, as in Uzbekistan, Hewitt also faced production challenges, although in this case it was the opposite situation. 'I wanted the printing to be "off" in appearance, but they always redo it to be perfect. I wanted the designs to look like my drawings, keeping the "hand"'.

While becoming a dealer and a designer, Hewitt continued her high-school enthusiasm for collecting. Despite her claims to be 'vaguely retired from collecting,' she acknowledges that her infatuation with certain objects is never too far from the surface. 'I was into hair dryers, so obviously I have a problem,' she says. In the late 1980s she upped her game and began collecting vintage Pucci, an Italian fashion designer, that she would pick up at flea markets – until the price went up. 'I have some pretty fabulous Pucci outfits that I can't fit any more.'

She fell in love, as she describes it, with Kütahya porcelain on her first trip to Turkey in the early nineties. She would go to the city of Bursa on every trip and return to the US with large quantities of antique turquoise ceramics. When she met her future husband,

Hüseyin Kaplan, his Kütahya collection certainly added to the attraction. They had both been collecting turquoise Kütahya for years. 'You could buy Kütahya for nothing,' she says, and she built what she describes as a nice collection of late 19th-century/early 20th-century turquoise and non-turquoise pieces. Then, as with many things she loved and collected, the price started to go up, up, up and she stopped buying it unless she found a choice piece for a steal.

Her most impressive collection, arguably, is of Kuznetsov plates made for the Central Asian markets. 'I was one of the first Western dealers to buy and sell them in the late 1990s. I started buying the ikat ones first – they were really rare.' She showed the first one she had bought in Uzbekistan to the dealers in Istanbul, asking them to save any they saw for her. When she returned from the US there were something like 100 plates waiting for her. 'I bought them all and brought them back to the US to sell. People were crazy for

them,' she says – because it was at the same time as the Goldman collection and the height of interest in ikat. When she moved to Istanbul from the US in 2003 she sold her private collection of around thirty ikat plates, many to her friend Victoria Rivers, who subsequently wrote a paper on them.[9] Dealers were still trying to sell her the ikat plates but they had become too expensive for Hewitt. When the price climbed to $250, she started buying other designs until their price also rose. When she started buying the floral plates, Kaplan also started buying them. 'If he sells one, he goes out and buys fifty – you can't find them any more because Hüseyin has them all!'

Hewitt is widely recognised for having spread the reputation of ikat far beyond the remote towns and villages of Uzbekistan where it was perfected centuries ago. Keith Recker of the International Folk Art Market suggests that the wide-ranging adaptation of ikat came

from people seeing Hewitt's successful work for de la Renta and Weinrib. She introduced high quality to the production of large quantities and original designs. Until then, the new ikat production was only for the domestic market. It used less silk, or was all cotton with more simple designs.[10]

Kate Fitz Gibbon credits Guido Goldman with exposing ikat to the West through the 1997 exhibition of his exquisite antique collection, and Hewitt with the revival of traditional ikat production, 'a technically difficult handicraft that equalled or surpassed, in technical quality and design sophistication, the 19th-century materials by replicating them in large quantities. This is practically the only time in the world where this has happened.'[11]

1   Now Thomas Jefferson University.

2   www.bhaktiziek.com

3   Jack Lenor Larsen (1927–2020) was a renowned textile designer, author, collector and promoter of traditional and contemporary craftsmanship.

4   Kate Fitz Gibbon and Andrew Hale. *Ikat: Splendid Silks of Central Asia: The Guido Goldman Collection*. Laurence King Publishing, 1997.

5   https://www.vogue.com/fashion-shows/spring-2005-ready-to-wear/oscar-de-la-renta/slideshow/collection

6   Tulu, or Tuylu in Turkish, literally means 'hairy'. Tulu rugs are characteristically long-piled and woven with large knots. 'Filikli' tulu rugs are made of the long, curly hair of Angora goats.

7   www.tulutextiles.com

8   www.shop-tamam.com

9   'Culture on a Platter: Politicization of Central Asian Ikat Patterns.' Victoria Z. Rivers. Textile Society of America Symposium Proceedings 2004. http://digitalcommons.unl.edu/cgi/viewcontent.cgi?article=1445&context=tsaconf

10 Keith Recker is creative director and board member of the International Folk Art Market. He is the author of *True Colors: World Masters of Natural Dyes and Pigments* and *Deep Color: The Shades that Shape Our Souls*, as well as the editor-in-chief and co-owner of *Table* magazine. Interview with the author.

11 See Andy Hale and Kate Fitz Gibbon, pp. 144 and 166.

Susan Gomersall

Like a rave

opener
Detail of an Anatolia tulu, 20th century, Susan Gomersall collection
opposite
Susan Gomersall
left
A woman weaving a jajim on her ground-loom (yer-hannasi) on the southern slopes of Mount Savalan, Iran, summer 1987

Photo by Nasrollah Kasraian, after Richard Tapper & Jon Thompson, eds., *The Nomadic Peoples of Iran*, Azimuth Editions, London 2002

'We thought we could do whatever we wanted.' That's what Susan Gomersall remembers thinking after she graduated in 1973 with a post-graduate degree in fine arts from the University of Reading in Berkshire, England. After fifty years of life as a rug dealer, it seems she was right.

'I didn't want to get a job, so I got a two-year scholarship from the British Council to study sculpture at the Polytechnic in Greece,' she says. It was a time when government money was flowing for young people looking for adventure, travel was cheap and borders were open. The scholarship turned out to be an unforeseen jumping-off point that led to her discovery of hand-woven kilims and carpets – an art form she didn't even know existed – and made pursuing them a lifetime passion.

Her story reflects the era that began in the 1960s and led to the opening up of previously little-known cultures to Western consumers, academics, museologists and collectors. The entry point was the woven and design traditions of these lesser-known territories. Through chance, and enormous daring, amid major political upheavals, Gomersall forged a life that brought together people from opposite sides of the world.

Gomersall's road to Kea Carpets and Kilims, her rug shops in Brooklyn (2001–19) and Hudson, New York (2011–present), began improbably, with the political turmoil in Greece in the early 1970s. For seven years the country was ruled by a series of military juntas that came to power through a coup d'état in 1967. By 1973 political opposition was heating up in Athens. Students at the Polytechnic, where Gomersall was studying, were actively organising against the junta, and all of the city was in chaos. It wasn't hard to see, her teacher Themias predicted, that there was going to be trouble.

Alarmed by the unrest and potential threat to her safety, the British Council gave Gomersall an ultimatum: come back to England or relocate to somewhere safer. 'Life has a way of throwing curve balls at you,' she says, 'and this was one of them.' With no appetite to return to England, she happily relocated to the town of Molyvos on the island of Lesvos, where she was to teach art classes for local students. There she met Brian, an Australian and the only other relocated international student on the island. The local students never showed up.

The two of them, without much to do, would sit and stare longingly across the water to southern Turkey, which was just a forty-minute boat ride away. Finally, they asked Themias for permission to go there, and he offered to join them. Turkey, with its long tradition of woven kilims, was home to some of the best in the world, and Themias happened to be an avid collector of them.

In Turkey, he drove them around looking at kilims in the seaside town of Ayvalık on the Aegean coast. 'I didn't even know what a kilim was – I'd never seen one in my life. They were so beautiful and I was enthralled,' she says. Kilims, as they're called in Turkey and Afghanistan, or gilim in Iran and kylym in Georgia, are flatwoven rugs that Gomersall contrasts with the pile or 'soft on the toes' rugs that most people are familiar with. They are a distinctive style of weaving used for centuries primarily in Turkey, Iran, Afghanistan and the Caucasus (Georgia, Armenia, Azerbaijan, Daghestan).

When it was time to return to Greece, Themias asked if they would take responsibility for the kilims that he had bought when they crossed the border. As foreigners, they weren't subject to the same taxes as Greeks, which meant Themias could avoid a high extra cost. Relations between Greece and Turkey had deteriorated sharply since 1974, when the Greek colonels had attempted a coup in Cyprus. In response, Turkey invaded Cyprus to protect the Turkish population living there. The resulting tension between the two countries led to the introduction of high export taxes for Greeks in Turkey, and a dispute that remains unresolved. It also meant that Gomersall, for the next two years, was regularly 'smuggling' kilims from Turkey to Greece and learning more and more about them with each trip.

She attributes her longstanding love of kilims and other rugs to Themias and those early years going to Turkey with him. He also introduced her to experts in Athens like Yanni Petsopoulos, author of one of the first books on flatweaves – *Kilims: Flat-Woven Tapestry Rugs* (1979) – and the British dealer David Black, whom she, and others, credit with introducing many types of rugs to the West.

Gomersall, who never formally studied rugs or textile design, says she gained her knowledge of them by buying, selling, touching and, in some cases, by smelling her way through thousands of them. When she first started visiting dealers in towns and villages from Turkey to Pakistan, very little was known about tribal carpets and information was scarce. She wasn't trained as an anthropologist yet, through her decades of fieldwork with nomads, she became an expert on their culture and weaving traditions. Her own book – *Kilim Rugs: Tribal Tales in Wool* – is an insider's introduction to tribal people, their lifestyles and the particular carpets and kilims associated with each tribe. It is clearly written by someone who has spent years getting to know the people and their carpets.

opposite
Detail of an Anatolian kilim, 20th century,
private collection

Photo by Nasrollah Kasraian, after Richard Tapper & Jon Thompson, eds., *The Nomadic Peoples of Iran*, Azimuth Editions, London 2002

At the time she was first introduced to kilims, not everyone saw their value the way she did. In the 19th century, the rug trade between Europe and the East had been prolific, but kilims retained second-class status. Western buyers preferred the thicker, more luxuriant, hand-knotted carpets. One particular dealer she met in Iran remarked disdainfully, 'That's what we wrap our [pile] rugs in when we ship them to the rest of the world.' Dealers of fine Persian pile carpets considered the kilims to be 'crap', she says.

There was an upside to such dismissiveness. Kilims didn't suffer the fate of pile carpets, whose colours and designs were altered and manipulated to keep pace with current trends. They are still being produced with patterns and motifs that can be traced back to antiquity.

After the British Council scholarship ended in 1975, Gomersall decided to remain in Greece. She rented an apartment in Athens for around $25 per month and, through what she describes as a 'fortunate accident', a ferry she was taking to visit some American friends on the island of Paros was forced to dock at the island of Kea on account of stormy weather. She ended up living there and, later, chose the name Kea when she set up her rug business in New York.

When her American friends, who became her business partners, decided to drive overland to India in 'Buttercup', their VW van, Gomersall was on board for the ride through Turkey, Iran, Afghanistan and Pakistan. 'That's how it all started,' she says, recalling her nomadic existence for the next twelve years, 'and it was so exciting!' One of her early experiences was an important lesson that proved invaluable over the years; and it helped her gain acceptance despite being an outsider in the countries she visited. A Canadian woman who was travelling with her decided to strip naked and jump into the Indus River. The locals who witnessed the

opposite
Family around a rug of their making, Iran, 1970s. Photo taken by Susan Gomersall's travel companion Jim Donnelly

above
A woman from one of the Turkic-speaking tribes whose summer pastures are on the slopes of Mount Alvand. On spring migration near Tuyserkan, Iran, 1986

display were 'furious with us', Gomersall says. From then on, she wore a shalwar kameez (long shirt over loose pants) and avoided aggravating members of cultures with more conservative values than her own laid-back sixties lifestyle.

'The biggest lesson, if you want to have a learning experience in another culture, is to understand that it's up to you to be accepted by those people, and not the other way around,' she says. The cultures and tribal people she met along the way captured her heart and her imagination. They led a 'true' nomadic life and made their living by buying and selling things they made or grew.

Gomersall's book gives many insights into this lifestyle, and part of the following is adapted from it. 'Self-sufficiency was the main aspect of nomadic life. Sheep and goats provide dairy products and meat, while their skins are used for clothes, shoes and shelter. Camels and horses, once the primary means of transportation, have been replaced by four-wheel drive trucks. Economic support from towns and cities provides markets for wool and livestock.'[1]

The routes that the tribes travelled became dotted with small villages and semi-permanent dwellings to meet the needs of nomads passing through. 'I have been to villages where everyone's occupation is connected to the rug trade,' she says. Villages with a plentiful water supply became centres for washing, shearing, spinning and dyeing. Larger towns and cities became market centres for buying and selling finished rugs. Some place names became identified with the rugs themselves.

There were tribal disputes from time to time, but with foreigners, she says, 'it was just peaceful, a very harmonious kind of feeling'. The Vietnam war was raging, and there were violent anti-war demonstrations all over the US and Europe. 'It was just such a relief to be at one with people.'

Her interest in tribal people, she says, was a two-way street, recalling that 'they were as interested in me as I was in them'. A whole village in northwestern Afghanistan came out 'to look at these freaks who'd rolled up in a bright orange Volkswagen bus'. They were invited into the local homes where she tasted food she'd never had before and learned to eat with her hands, which, she discovered is 'such a satisfying thing to do. You'll never get fat if you eat with your hands.'

As a female rug dealer, Gomersall was often invited into the kitchens of the wives and sisters of the male dealers she worked with. 'They would make fun of my clothing and tease me, but I was a source of income for them, helping the family a lot.' She became like a sister and they taught her how to cook their dishes. In Pakistan, the younger women could all speak English and they would translate for her when necessary.

Many of her assumptions were proved wrong once she entered the women's circle and saw how things were done. 'I assumed that weaving traditions were passed from mothers to daughters, but in fact the skill

opposite
Detail of a Central Anatolian kilim,
19th century, private collection

above
Shesh Baylu (Shesh Boluki) women
weaving a knotted-pile carpet near
Shirin Cheshmeh, Iran, summer 1989

and the traditional patterns jump from grandmothers to granddaughters.' The wives and mothers, she learned, were too busy running daily life to do much of the teaching, although they would do some of the weaving.

She found that the women were strong and independent despite their separation, in public, from male society and other limitations. Although, as she puts it, 'they may not be able to walk around in mini-skirts, and if they want to leave it's hard, because that's the culture they were born into', but, she stresses, they had a strong community within a community.

Being welcomed into the domestic domain allowed Gomersall to see, first-hand, how kilims were made and used in daily life. 'It is a cover for your bed, your table, your overcoat on a cold night.' Bags that were made to carry the tent walls were later used as storage bags for rice and wheat. They were hung horizontally around the tent to provide insulation as well as colour, and over the entranceway as a door.

With limited funds it made sense for Gomersall and her travel companions to become traders themselves, despite how foreign a nomadic lifestyle was to her own past. That was the culture she was living in, and it suited her happy-go-lucky attitude. 'I didn't have a ten-year plan, not even a ten-day plan beyond staying healthy and having enough money to buy and sell,' she says. 'We were just really optimistic.'

The camaraderie of fellow travellers on the road was a big part of the experience. It was also the best way to learn the trade, with information flowing freely whether you were from Italy or Indiana. 'You'd be sitting in a guesthouse and you'd be talking to someone and they'd say, oh, have you been to Isfahan? They have fabulous stuff there. And you should look up my friend so and so... Everything was word of mouth, everyone talked to each other.' If she didn't know something about a rug, she'd ask another dealer about it, and return the favour when she could. 'I'd also give them a ballpark of what they could expect to sell it for on the European market.'

In the beginning they bought small things that were easy to transport, like locally made jewellery, embroideries, and 'exotic' artefacts that they would sell in Europe. The profits supported the next overland trip to India, where Gomersall hung out in the winter until she could head back overland in the warm spring weather, picking up items along the way to trade back in Greece.

As the 'merchant gene' developed, she noticed that the major commodity of the tribal peoples was their weavings, beautiful works of art which were just everyday objects to them. They had huge flocks of sheep and every family had a loom. They also wove knotted carpets, not only kilims, using geometric and abstracted animal and floral details as designs in both types. The pile rugs were made primarily for sale and trade while kilims were made for home use such as trappings for horses or containers for cooking utensils, or wraps for precious objects such as a family's copy of the Qur'an. Tribal people, she learned, created textiles that could serve all the functional needs they had; they could also be folded and stacked for

left
Anatolian tulu, 20th century, Susan Gomersall collection
opposite, above
Trading yarn for staples like wheat and rice, Iran, 1970s. Photo taken by Susan Gomersall's travel companion Jim Donnelly

opposite, below
Women cooking, Iran, 1970s. Photo taken by Susan Gomersall's travel companion Jim Donnelly

easy transport from one encampment to the next, since every aspect of nomadic life had to be fluid.

There were markets where everybody would meet to trade whatever they had. 'They traded their rugs to each other for wheat, animals and other commodities and very happily sold them to us for American dollars,' she says. 'It was like a tribal rave – fabulous blow-outs full of noise and colour!'

Soon she and her partner were right in the swing of trading. Sony Walkmans, popular at the time in the West, would buy a lot of jewellery and a few carpets, which they sold to boutiques all over Greece while they could still travel back and forth overland. That changed in 1979 with the revolution in Iran and Soviet tanks rolling into Afghanistan. Borders were closed and they were forced to fly, rather than drive, back to Greece, which limited what they could bring back to sell: just jewellery.

Later she tried to legally import carpets to Greece, along with the jewellery, but couldn't work the 'fakelaki' system which involved slipping an 'envelope' of cash under the table to the customs officer.[2] If there wasn't enough 'laki' (dollars) in the envelope, you didn't get your rugs. At one point customs officers, knowing they were selling rugs to the boutiques for the summer tourist trade, held up the carpets for almost the whole summer. It almost bankrupted them.

This was the last straw for Gomersall's business partners, a husband and wife who by then had a child; they decided to return to the US and settle down. Soon after, Gomersall also left Greece. In 1986 she began to fully develop her business, importing carpets directly to the US. Coming to the US, she says, was the first time she actually had a fully legitimate business, because in Greece it had been possible to avoid paying taxes.

above
Woman weaving, Iran, 1970s. Photo taken by Susan Gomersall's travel companion Jim Donnelly

opposite
Shirvan 'racing car' kilim, last quarter 19th century. Art Institute of Chicago, 2012.578, Gift of Barbara Bluhm-Kaul, Neil Bluhm, and Family

119

Pakistan, in those years, was the hub for rugs from all over the region – Uzbekistan, Azerbaijan, Iran, Turkmenistan. These countries, which were part of the USSR, were closed for travel to Westerners during the 'Cold War'. The western Pakistani cities of Peshawar and Quetta were the best markets because rugs came directly across the nearby Afghan and Iran borders. Pakistan also had 'favoured nation' status with the US, which made it easy and inexpensive to import rugs from there.

To find good rugs, Gomersall needed to hook up with a Pakistani picker – someone who would act as a scout to locate the best places and people who had carpets to sell. It didn't take long before she found one. 'I'd stay in a little hotel in Peshawar and I'd wander around the tiny bazaar there. I saw this fabulous stall that had really good-looking kilims so I walked in and came across Hanif and his beautiful rugs and beautiful prices.'

Hanif and his son, Zaman, became her pickers. Their range of rugs – Iranian, Turkmen, Afghan – were from places where she could no longer go herself. They had people collecting them in each country and bringing them back to Pakistan. 'I would travel with Hanif and Zaman to Peshawar, Quetta, and villages along the way, selecting the carpets I liked for export to the US.'

When she first came to the US, before she opened a shop, she would set up a booth at trade shows. Tribal rugs were relatively new to the American market but their aesthetic and price point 'went wonderfully with all those hard wood floors' at a time when wall-to-wall carpets were on the way out and area rugs were the new fashion.

The kilims were so unfamiliar that people would ask her which side of the rug was the front. The shape of kilims, which are usually long and narrow, is difficult for Westerners, unfamiliar with tribal life, to understand. Not only were they woven on narrow looms, but most Central Asian village houses had just one narrow room. Since there was no market in Europe for kilims until the latter half of the 19th century, very few Western-sized kilims were made, aside from those produced by certain tribal groups for ceremonial occasions or as gifts to the mosques. Nomads might spread a long, slender kilim on the ground in order to sleep on it, or use a square sofreh kilim to wrap around bread to keep it warm and then use it as a cloth to put the food on.

With no internet or social media yet in the 1980s, Gomersall had to rely on word of mouth to let people know about her carpets. Friends in the US who were 'turned on by something they'd never come across before' helped her by inviting people to their homes to see the rugs. A group of Harvard professors and literary people were so moved by the rugs that word about them soon spread from Cambridge, MA, to New York and Pennsylvania. People loved the experience of buying from someone who actually went out and bought the rugs where they were made and knew

above
A wool-dresser or bow-carder
(hallaj) with his bow and mallet
prepares raw wool for felt making,
Iran, 1980s

the stories behind them. 'It was ground-breaking. I was finding and bringing beautiful pieces of art in the form of rugs and kilims that people hadn't seen before.'

By the late 1990s, kilims had become part of the popular 'bohemian chic' design trend. They were in all the interior design magazines and designers were using them often. Gomersall continued to travel back and forth to Turkey and Pakistan, working with her pickers to buy more kilims, but their popularity wasn't the only thing motivating her. 'I loved the lifestyle – the people I met on the road, both foreigners and the local pickers, the dealers,' she says. Many of these locals were shocked that Westerners would buy a kilim which they thought had no international value at all.

As she established her business in the US, dramatic changes were unfolding, over the years, in the countries where she bought carpets. During the 1980s, after the Iran revolution and the Russian invasion of Afghanistan, there was a large influx of refugees to the US from countries in the region. Many moved to places like New Mexico and California, where the climate was similar to that of their own countries. Others, whom Gomersall had known in Peshawar, came to New York, opening their own carpet shops and providing Gomersall, among others, with repair and specialised cleaning services for their imported carpets.

In addition to all the political upheaval, new technology also brought changes. Long-held cultural traditions suddenly no longer applied. In the early 1990s, Gomersall was caught off-guard when she was staying in a hotel in Pakistan that, for the first time, had television with foreign stations. One night Zaman, her picker, knocked on her door and asked. 'Mr Susan [as she was called], can I come into your room to watch a TV programme?' The use of the masculine prefix was commonly used to address Western women, since they didn't fit the traditional female stereotype in Pakistan. 'Are you mad?' she replied, reminding Zaman that his father had always insisted that no male could ever come into her room. He apologised profusely.

Until then her male pickers had always been very careful to guard her room to make sure that no one broke in. They would never have knocked on the door because they didn't want anybody saying that she was a prostitute. In the conservative Pakistani society, any private contact between men and women was immediately suspect. After this incident she knew that the advent of television and other soon-to-follow technological changes would have a big impact.

The last time Gomersall was in Pakistan, just before 9/11, she found that a group of pickers she worked with there were very nervous. There were certain places she wanted to go but, they told her, 'No, Mr Susan, we can't go there, it's not friendly.' Anti-American feelings were being whipped into a frenzy on the internet. Daniel Pearl, an American journalist, was kidnapped

and later beheaded by terrorists in Sindh in February, 2001. After 9/11 anti-American sentiment grew even more hostile and travel by Westerners in Pakistan was increasingly dangerous.

Other big, more positive changes were also underway. She met and partnered with New York carpet designer Azy Schecter and, in 2001, Kea Kilims became Kea Carpets and Kilims, combining contemporary and tribal carpets under one roof in a newly opened store in Brooklyn.

With the growing dangers of travel after 9/11, it was technology that enabled them to continue importing rugs from Pakistan and Afghanistan, where they risked being kidnapped or caught in a terrorist attack. Their long-time picker in Turkey, who had come to understand their taste over many years working with Gomersall, would send photos online of carpet collections he had put together for them, offering advice on which carpets were very old or 'newish'. According to them, he never sent anything that disappointed.

In response to the interest in the stories behind the carpets, Gomersall and Schecter began to write them up. This helped collectors and customers better understand what they were looking at and appreciate why, for example, they didn't come in standard sizes. As we've seen, tribal rugs are made for purposes other than floor covering, but that is how they're primarily used in the West. Gomersall and Schecter showed customers how to utilise unique tribal carpets creatively in a contemporary Western setting rather than trying to replicate a standardised area rug or create a wall-to-wall effect.

Yet more changes followed in the wider world, some good, some challenging. New markets opened up in Central Asia, after the fall of the Soviet Union in 1991, which led to discoveries like Uzbek julkhyrs ('bearskins'), tribal 'sleeping bags' made from a combination of sheep and yak wool. 'We bought about five of them and they sold immediately.'

Soaring rents in New York City forced Kea Carpets and Kilims, after sixteen years in the same premises, to close its Brooklyn shop in 2019. The upstate operation in Hudson, NY, continues with a strong online presence.

After fifty years of buying and selling tribal carpets, Gomersall still gets animated talking about them. The passion she felt on seeing them for the first time in Turkey, many decades ago, hasn't waned. It propelled her not only to a life of travel and adventure importing beautiful carpets, but also to becoming an ambassador for the cultures that produce them.

1   Adapted from Gomersall, *Kilim Rugs: Tribal Tales in Wool*, Schiffer 1999.
2   In Greek, the word 'fakelaki' literally means 'little envelope'. But symbolically, the word is used in Greek jargon to refer to the slipping of bribes to public servants and private companies by citizens in order to expedite goods and services.

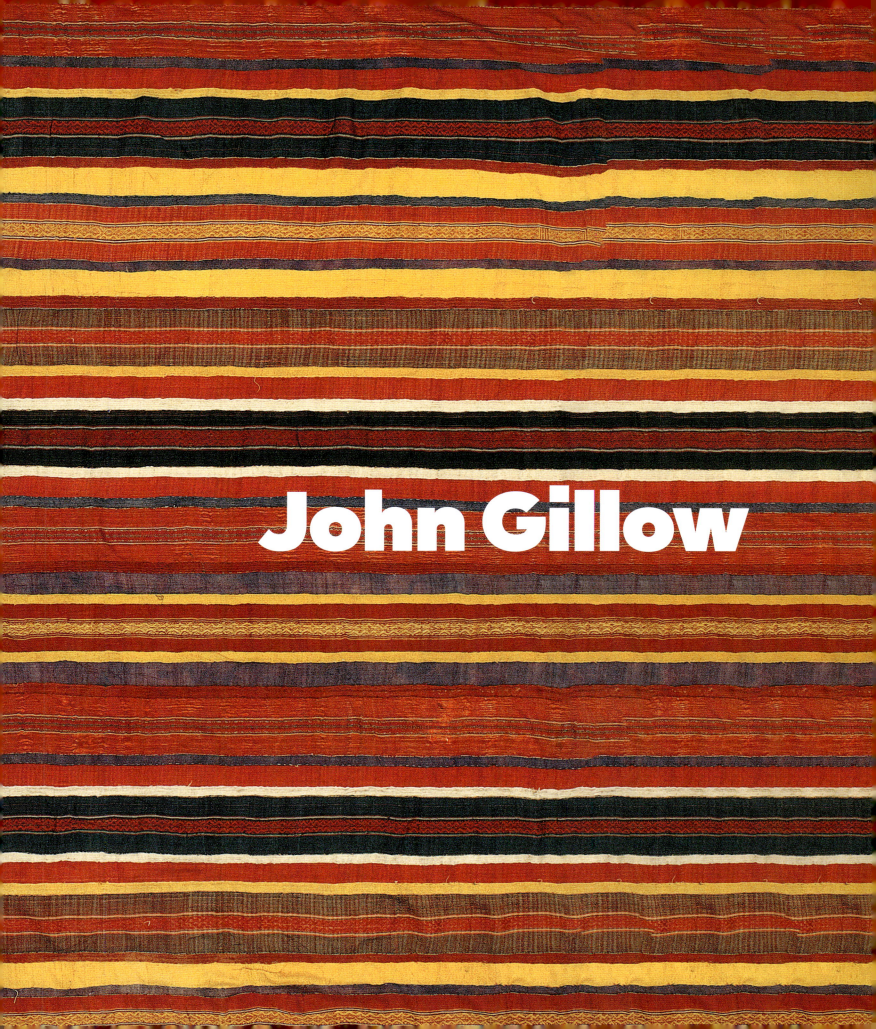

John Gillow

Travelling in the blood

Everybody was moving in '68. After reading Jack Kerouac and smoking a joint, you just wanted to head east. I went hitchhiking around Europe with my cousin. Later that year, back in Britain, I worked on a hop farm for the brewing industry. There was a long-haired hippie working there and he told me about Istanbul. My schoolboy eyes widened and I thought, am I gonna go there?

The following summer I set off for Istanbul. I was going to hitch hike but my mother made sure I went by train. I arrived at night and the European railway station looked just like it did in the Lawrence of Arabia movie which I had watched when I was twelve. There were great heaps of garbage, one-eyed mangy cats sitting on top spitting, and Turkish boys with shaved heads barking 'one two three lira you stay at my place'. It was a little bit intimidating.

I woke up in the middle of my first night and heard the muezzin's call to prayer. I sat up on the mattress I had in this cheap dive. All the hackles and the hair on my neck were bristling and I thought 'here I am!'

The old ladies were very kind. They looked after you – 'You can sleep here, don't talk to that man, here's something to eat.' It was my first exposure to the Muslim world and I liked it. I thought the hospitality, generosity and kindness were amazing.

I walked around the Grand Bazaar and there were carpets and furs and silver. All kinds of things that a young schoolboy couldn't afford. Then I came across scraps of Ottoman embroidery. I bought those – they were ten bob each – for presents for my girlfriend, sister, doting grandmother. I got hooked on the textiles themselves but I also wanted to find out more about the nomads and peasants who'd made them.

There were people flooding back from India who had set off with ten quid in their pocket. They told me all these stories. I realised that the world was not a threatening place and decided that after I graduated I would make some money and travel.'

— John Gillow

Collecting and dealing textiles allowed John Gillow to do what he loves and to do what he must do – travel and earn a living to support his growing family. It took him a number of years to find a way to do both, despite having what he calls 'travelling in my blood'. Cambridge based, he is now a master storyteller, inveterate traveller, prolific author, international textile dealer and a globally recognised expert in his field.

Gillow's childhood helped prepare him for the itinerant life he was to lead. In the 1950s, when he was eleven years old, his father worked for the Maltese government. Malta, a Mediterranean archipelago of islands fifty miles south of Italy, is now independent, but was then still a British colony. 'I went to a Maltese school, I was in a Maltese scout troop, I spoke a bit of Maltese,' he remembers.

He began to study science in the autumn of 1969, eventually obtaining a Master of Science degree in irrigation engineering, which proved to be a considerable detour on the path to what he would ultimately do. During summer school breaks he continued to pursue his love of travel, even if it didn't always go as planned. Hitch hiking, in 1970, to the Moroccan border, he was denied entry owing to his long hair. 'I was so vain I refused to cut it,' he says, learning, the hard way, the fundamental rule for travellers that 'when in Rome, do as the Romans'.

In the 1971 summer break Gillow travelled, unwittingly, to places experiencing intense political tension, starting in what was then known as the Socialist Federal Republic of Yugoslavia (SFRY). It was still under the leadership of Marshal Josip Broz Tito, with feared secret police.

An ongoing movement to increase the powers of the individual federated republics had led to the 'Croatian Spring', soon crushed by Tito's forces. None of this political turmoil registered on the young Gillow, nor did it deter his return, from there, to Istanbul where he saw more clashes between communist elements and the fascists who were in power at the time. 'The army was goose-stepping on the main street. Every other bookshop was selling Hitler's *Mein Kampf*. It was kind of shocking to me but I just thought, that's the way it is. It didn't affect me or the way people treated me. My ability to move around was my wonderful hot currency,' he maintains, ignoring the fact that being a foreigner may also have protected him, along with just plain luck.

By this point, Gillow started to realise that he wanted travelling to be his life and everything else to be subordinate to that. Collecting and dealing, as a way to sustain his passion for travel, came later, when earning a living wasn't as easy as it was in those early days of the 1970s. 'You could just get up in the morning and get a reasonably well-paying job. Your money in Western currency was worth an awful lot and you could live for a very long time on a very little,' he says.

Easy money didn't necessarily mean a lot of money and, while travelling East was often cheap, it wasn't luxurious. Gillow's strong urge to travel superseded desire for the comforts of home. 'We were prepared to really rough it. We slept in flea-ridden dives and we travelled on buses and hitch hiked when we could. We learned to live very cheaply,' he says, noting that a nineteen-month trip in 1974 with his wife cost a total of £1,000 for the two of them. 'We went from London through Iran, Afghanistan and Pakistan to India, where we stayed for six months. Then we caught a boat from Sri Lanka to Durban, to visit my father who was working in Lesotho and, finally, we travelled across Africa all the way from the Cape to Cairo.'

Arriving in South Africa, Gillow was again confronted by a political situation he wasn't prepared for. A boycott movement, which became international, had been established in 1959 to protest against the apartheid treatment of black South Africans. It was not lifted until September 1993 after South Africa was set on the path to democratic elections. 'The portly customs officer came on board the ship in his white cap and colonial white shorts and socks. All he said to us was. "Do you have any *Playboy* magazines?" I said "No". He said "Welcome to South Africa" and stamped my passport. I was so shocked I let him.' He later had to get a supplementary passport in Lesotho without the stamp so he could continue to travel in other African countries that were boycotting South Africa.

Back in England in 1976, with a baby on the way, Gillow realised he needed to make a sustainable living. He had recently seen Joss Graham's first exhibition of embroidery from Sindh, Pakistan (he acknowledges Graham's influence and credits him with being the first to recognise the appeal of embroidery from the region). 'So, I buggered off back to India, bought a few things and brought them back to sell.'

When he saw that people would buy them, he went back to India again the next year, on a break from his studies, and bought more. Travelling back and forth overland, Gillow visited Iran several times in the years before and just after the 1979 revolution. Unlike many Westerners who whizzed through, or avoided the country altogether on account of the growing anti-Western atmosphere, Gillow got to know the merchants.

His lack of concern about being in a hostile environment grew from seeing his parents' experience in places like Lebanon where they had gone at the height of the civil war in 1976. His father,

opposite
Russian rollerprint made for the
Iranian market

Gillow says, dealt with danger without batting an eyelid. For Gillow, travelling in dangerous places was just something the family did. His height of 6ft 3in, in such situations, was a noticeable asset.

Iran in the 1970s saw a series of events that culminated in the abolition of the monarchy. Mohammad Reza Pahlavi, the last Shah of Iran, was replaced with an Islamic republic under the Grand Ayatollah Ruhollah Khomeini, in a revolution supported by various Islamist and leftist movements united, in part, by a hatred of the West. By now Gillow had started to understand that there was often more going on in the places he visited than met the eye. Unperturbed by the potential danger of a Westerner poking around in a distinctly anti-Western environment, he welcomed opportunities to learn more. 'I was buying things and talking to the merchants about textiles. Then they would close the door and talk about politics, open the door and talk about textiles again,' he says, alluding to the risk for anyone, including himself, caught openly discussing the political situation.

The stopovers in Iran provided more than a lesson in current affairs. The country had a centuries-long history in the production and trade of textiles and carpets – the exchange of weavers, dyers, design motifs and material goods – including long-established dealings with India. Gillow learned a lot from the local dealers.

From 1974–78 Gillow travelled to Afghanistan in a series of three trips that took him to Herat, Kandahar, Kabul, Mazar-i-Sharif and down to Peshawar in Pakistan near the Afghan border. He liked Afghans, but he wasn't enthralled with the 'hip scene' of Westerners he discovered in Kabul, which had become the main way station along the hippie trail. More of a loner than most of them, Gillow thought that, 'There were too many foreigners wearing leather trousers and smoking big joints, bragging about themselves and how hip they were and how much dope they had stashed.'

That unappealing scene to him, along with his view that things in Kabul were either ludicrously cheap or ludicrously expensive, meant that Afghanistan never became a favourite destination – especially when he hadn't yet the confidence or knowledge to work out who was selling which of the two extremes. The 1979 Russian invasion of Afghanistan was another big deterrent for him. Some dealers who were already well established in the country, like Pip Rau, did well working in a conflict zone, particularly when others were reluctant to go there, meaning less competition.

His desire for a life of travel was tested, just before the Russian invasion, when he got an offer of an engineering job in Afghanistan on the Helmand River irrigation scheme. Despite a growing family

above
Elaborate wooden balconies in the Old
Town of Peshawar, Pakistan
opposite
Bethlehem dress panel of couched
cording and silk embroidery on taffeta

and the on-going need to put food on the table he fully decided, after toying with the offer, that he didn't want the job. By 1980 he had a clear understanding of what he did want. He set off to the district of Kutch in the Indian state of Gujarat. 'I had two children. I wanted to keep travelling to India, so I had to make it work,' he says, summarising a more focused approach to being a dealer. He was determined to learn more about the culture and develop a reliable network of pickers to help find and buy the unique textiles of the region.

'Kutch then was just incredible,' he recalls, describing what he encountered in the walled capital city of Bhuj. 'I stayed in a hotel called Juntagar, which means People's House. It was owned by a very rich Jain who sat in a deck chair not saying a word, in front of a poster of Marx, Engels, Lenin and Mao.'

Gillow was awestruck as he wandered the bazaar encountering the diversity of people and their unique styles of dress and distinctive ornamentation. 'There were Jats, a community with pastoral origins in the Indus Valley near the Pakistan border, with henna-dyed beards, block-printed ajrakh turbans and men in longhis [an uncut cloth wrapped around the waist]. The Jat women had nose rings that were so heavy they were attached by a cord to their hair. There were Sidis, people of African descent, who had been brought over as slaves to serve the local Rajahs.'

He soon met some Vagris, a low caste of rag pickers who lived by the rubbish dump and collected embroideries from the surrounding villages. 'We used to drink tea – that was very important. They were flattered that I would drink tea with them, which members of castes higher than them wouldn't do. I got friendly with one who was younger than me – a plump, jolly chap – and I'd buy embroideries from him.' As well as sourcing embroideries, Gillow's new friend also became an important fund of information about what he was buying and the people who made it. 'He'd tell me which village each piece was from and which caste had made it, so I built up a picture of how Kutch worked, and I would travel around buying textiles.'

Gillow's growing knowledge and experience gave him rare access and insight into the life of the lower castes he was meeting – Vagri, Rabari, Arya – and the role of textiles in their families. 'It was stuff various castes made for their dowries. They create a trousseau for a girl. The girl herself will do the embroidery and anyone who is good with a needle will contribute. They make a backless bodice called choli, a full skirt or ghagra, a dupatta shawl, a toran, which is a curtain hanging above a doorway, chakla squares, embroidered and beaded, covers for quilts and quilts – everything for the wedding. They also make additional, plainer clothes for everyday use.'

An outsider buying textiles required a good understanding of the complexities that had to be navigated in an unfamiliar world. Gillow

above
John Gillow on his travels in the 1970s
opposite
Khouri khanum ('Sun Maiden') sequin embroideries, Isfahan district, Iran

Photograph by Luke Gillow, Tasmin Beedle and James Austin from *Textiles of the Islamic World* published by Thames & Hudson Ltd., London

witnessed the confusion caused when his wife accompanied him on one of his trips, with the local women wondering why his wife was looking to buy pieces rather than embroider them herself.

Gillow never bought directly from the village women in their homes, working instead through the Vagris, who would collect the textiles and bring them to him. 'If you go into a house and you try to buy something, the price they initially demand will be high and you have to haggle it down,' he explains. 'I'm a good bargainer, but I think it's very crass to haggle with a person on something they've made themselves.'

Gillow was well aware of the economic differences between where he was buying textiles and where he was selling them. The trade benefited both parties to the transaction, he says, despite the big differences between the two countries. 'What makes you feel good is that you're actually looking after your suppliers. You're providing them money that they're using to feed their children, and the money gets spread around through the network of runners.'

Once at a teahouse Gillow met an older Rabari woman who couldn't understand why he was buying her textiles. Eventually, she asked the man who ran the teashop who the foreigner was. Expecting the owner to say he was an Englishman, Gillow was amused to hear himself referred to as a Vagri, or rag and bone man. It did not seem that inappropriate an image when, on the flight home, Gillow would shove underneath his seat big bags stuffed with his purchases.

Once he made the decision to give full-time dealing a go, it took a while before Gillow could count on being able to support his growing family. 'When my children were small it was very much a question of living hand to mouth. I'd make twenty quid for the weekend – that was our money for the week.' He was bringing back textiles and carpets for which there was not yet much awareness or demand. Some of the other traders opened shops to sell their imports. Gillow had to look for other ways to find customers, demonstrating, once again, his determination to make viable his chosen lifestyle and to support his family.

Starting close to home, he began by using his house as an outlet to sell items he'd bought in India; friends and neighbours would come and buy things for as little as £5. Two or three times a year he'd put on exhibitions at the local wholefood shop. 'You could sell stuff very cheaply then and still make a reasonable profit, although the returns, at first, were meagre.'

Soon Gillow found himself selling at the local East Anglian fairs, with their music, theatre and circus acts along with stalls for selling crafts and other goods like Gillow's imports. He found the experience highly enjoyable. Held on various weekends between 1978 and 1986, the fairs have been described as an 'eclectic mix of hippies, bikers, punks and the general public gathered to live an "alternative lifestyle" for the weekend. Camping facilities were always somewhat basic... the music was

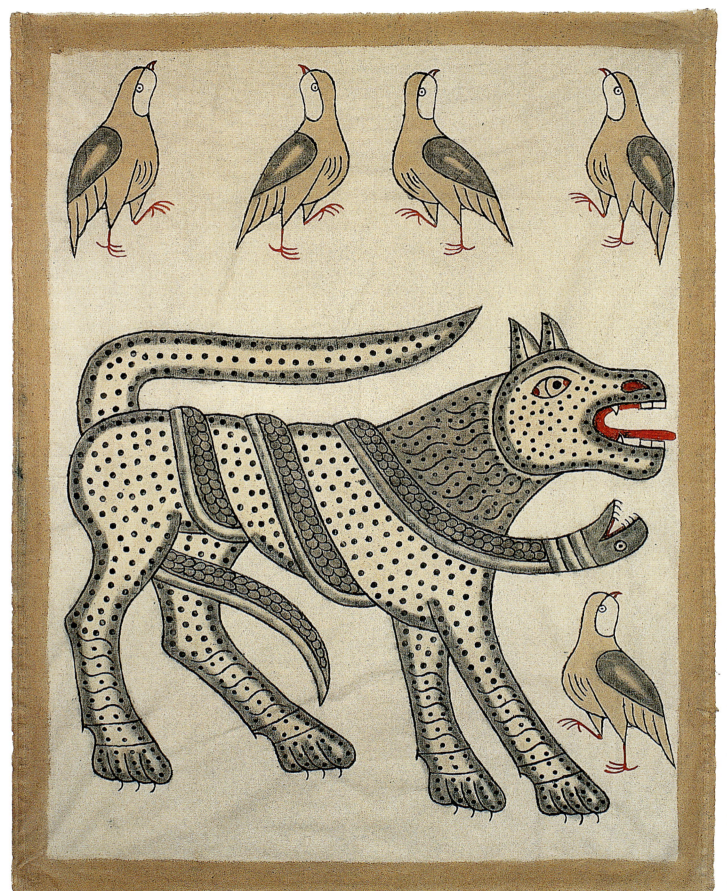

Photograph by Luke Gillow, Tasmin Beedle and James Austin from *Textiles of the Islamic World* published by Thames & Hudson Ltd., London

sometimes dodgy, there were often far more naked people than [one] really wanted to encounter ... but the real ale was always plentiful.'[1]

With Prime Minister Margaret Thatcher in power in the UK from 1979–1990, Gillow had to confront the tough financial impact of domestic politics. Thatcher's Conservative policies of austerity meant that people spent their money on necessities, not exotic items that they didn't actually need, like the ones he was selling.

Around this time, he started lecturing and exhibiting at art colleges. When Marianne Straub – a Swiss weaver and one of the leading textile designers in Britain from 1940–1960 – started to buy from him, others at the colleges followed her lead. 'I think they liked the textiles because they recognised the art in it,' he says, adding that it was almost exclusively women who bought the best ones.

After another chance encounter with Joss Graham, Gillow decided to go to Pakistan, after Graham confided that 'the best stuff is in Sindh, especially Tharparkar'. Graham had been an early visitor, one of the few, to that part of the country. Arriving in Karachi Gillow encountered a virtual civil war underway between two of the main ethnic groups in the city, who were political rivals: the Muhajirs (Urdu-speaking refugees from India after the 1947 Partition of India and Pakistan) and the Pashtuns (Pashtu speakers from the north west, many of whom were fleeing the civil war in Afghanistan).

When the Pashtuns he met learned that he was British, they challenged him to justify why Britain had allowed Altaf Hussain, the founder and leader of the Muttahida Qaumi Movement, made up of Muhajirs, to immigrate to Britain – they regarded the MQM as a mafia-style political party. Hussain had fled to London in 1991 after an attempt on his life in Karachi. Gillow had never heard of him.

Leaving behind the riots and carnage in Karachi, Gillow moved to the nearby Thar Desert (also known as Tharparkar) – a 77,000-square-mile wilderness that forms a natural boundary between India and Pakistan. His guide was a man called Geena, from the Meghwal, a low caste known for their outstanding embroidery. Art and artisan crafts have been part of Thar society for centuries. Local creativity encompasses appliquéd rilli quilts, pottery, puppet-making, carpet-making, traditional decoration, block printing and cobbling, in addition to embroidery. In the township of Chachro alone, along the southeast border between Pakistan and India, there are 6,000 handlooms.

The district of Tharparkar was traditionally around 80 per cent Hindu, until Partition in 1947 caused many of these people to migrate to India. Tharparkar is still home to a Hindu majority, however, and the caste structure is strong. Much of the fine embroidery produced by the Meghwal is executed for the landowning upper class, who are mainly Muslim.

opposite
Printed and painted 'hunting cloth'
from Herat, Afghanistan
right
Travel memorabilia from across
the world

Gillow and Geena travelled together by bus to the city of Umerkot, picked up a jeep, and drove off-road to try to avoid the army and police who were stationed at various points, owing to the political unrest. A chance encounter at a crossroads wasn't what they expected. 'A bald, tall, skinny chap wearing a Baluchi cap was stretched out on a charpoy.[2] He got up when our jeep stopped, and barked, in faultless English, "Where are you from?"' When Gillow replied that he was British, the officer repeated the question. 'Cambridge,' said Gillow. 'I'm from the other place,' the officer replied, assuming Gillow understood he meant Oxford University, well known as the Cambridge rival. 'You can go anywhere in my district,' he told Gillow in a gesture of sincere, though meaningless, camaraderie. As Gillow says, the army would never have allowed it. They stayed in Geena's village, pulling up water, by hand, from 200 feet down with the help of women and boys tugging on ropes.

Gillow also travelled to Peshawar, a northwestern Pakistani city close to the Afghan border, where he felt an affinity with the Pashtuns who lived there. 'I love Peshawar. It's the winter capital of Afghanistan,' he says, harkening to the mid-1800s when this northwest province, now called Khyber Pakhtunkhwa, was part of British colonial Afghanistan.

When the situation for Westerners in Pakistan became dangerous after 9/11, Gillow's suppliers offered to get him shalwar kameez – the traditional dress worn by Pashtun men – but he declined, fearing it would only create suspicion. Being transparent, he believes, is the best way to operate when travelling, even in dangerous situations. 'If you behave in an honest manner you'll get respect and you'll get friends. I've got friends, particularly in Pakistan, whom I would trust my life to.'

Despite his years of experience in the country, Gillow could still be surprised. When an older Afghan woman came into a teashop in Peshawar with her granddaughter, she was introduced as a runner – someone who went door to door finding textiles for sale. Only then did he realise that all the runners for the Afghan merchants he dealt with were women, not men as he had previously thought. 'You're just brainwashed that Afghanistan is a totally male-dominated society. But it's the women who are the collectors. Women aren't going to let a man into the house and start pulling open their drawers.'

When he felt a degree of financial security from his Indian and Pakistani business, Gillow branched out to countries in Africa that he had visited twenty years earlier. In 1994, he went back to Ghana with his eleven-year-old son. He was looking for narrow strip-loom weaves made by the Asante and Ewe tribes. After initially buying the brightly coloured kente cloths woven by the Asante in Accra's main market, he headed for the mostly Muslim Nima market, in a less affluent area known for its peaceful cultural and religious diversity, where he found 'subtler and more fun' cloths woven by the Ewe.

akg-images / Jean-Louis Nou

above
Villager in the Thar Desert on her way to the well, 1977
opposite
Memon woman's embroidered **aba**, Kutch, India

above

Spice merchants in the bazaar in
Peshawar, May 1984

Describing the light-hearted approach to negotiating there, he says, 'You haggle over the price and they make a joke.' He admired how he could confidently walk, late at night, anywhere in Accra and 'the worst that will happen is you'll get on the bible track', referring to the large presence of Christian evangelicals.

His constant search for fresh textiles took him to remote territories like Sumatra, one of 17,000 islands that make up Indonesia, after a friend told him that Indonesia had a great transport system and that you could fly anywhere in the country. 'I was finding absolutely amazing things there,' he says, acknowledging the support of Thomas Murray, who, he says, 'was always floating around Indonesia and was always very good to me'.

Gillow first met Murray in San Francisco at a tribal art fair, a group of dealers that initially coalesced in 1985 to create a market that continues to the present day. He was at first hesitant to travel, at considerable expense, to an event somewhere he was unknown. But in the late 1990s he agreed to go, so as to investigate expanding his British client base.

Gillow offered a level of textile that appealed, and was affordable, to a large sector, whereas others searched exclusively for museum-quality materials requiring elite customers who could afford them. The high end of the textile trade didn't interest Gillow who, by his own account, was 'not good with the rich... I find myself being rude to them. I'm not interested in anybody who wants to buy something for an investment. Don't come to me,' he says.

Although he likes a bargain as much as the next person, he says he's not interested in a textile as a unit of value. 'I buy it because I like it and I'm interested in the people who are selling it.' On a trip to Hainan Island, off the coast of China, Gillow tried to explain how he likes to 'sniff out a place' to his son who, after an hour of seemingly mindless wandering, asked his dad exactly what they were looking for. 'I said we're looking for a market, and we're going to go into the market, and at the back there's going to be a man or woman sitting on a great untidy heap of textiles and when we find that place and that person, we've found it!'

For Gillow, the hunt itself has been part of the thrill. It has sometimes led to unexpected but valuable discoveries, as it did in Gujarat. After wandering aimlessly in the heat for a couple of hours, looking for someone he couldn't find, he was about to give up. 'All of a sudden, this man grabs me by the arm. He walks me down one street, then a side street, still tightly gripping my arm. He bangs loudly on a door. This stout little man with stubble opens the door and says to come in, where there's around 30,000 textiles. I spent a couple of nights going through a lot of textiles,' he says. 'That joy of finding a reliable family to deal with, I still really love that.'

From early on, Gillow shared his love of dealing, and what he has learned from it, with almost anyone interested. Although he had a good

response to his early lectures at the local wholefood shop in Cambridge, he admits he was nervous and lacked confidence. Once he discovered he could entertain an audience, it became one of the things he enjoys most. 'I go through textiles, and talk about technique, and then I digress and talk about Afghan marital habits or ask why we went to war in Afghanistan.' This free-wheeling style of lecturing has made him highly sought-after on the textile lecture circuit. 'A living conduit whose knowledge connects history to place and cloth' is how Gillow was introduced at a 2018 symposium in Vancouver.

Gillow was travelling in Indonesia when author Nicholas Barnard asked him to collaborate on writing a book on Indian textiles. Gillow presumed that he would do the research and Barnard would write it, but, owing to unanticipated personal complications for Barnard, Gillow ended up writing a good portion of it. 'I realised then I could actually do it,' he says.

When his wife left him he desperately needed a project to occupy him, which writing books provided. 'I was so angry I used to get up at 4 a.m. to write,' he says, adding that becoming an author educated him. 'If you write one book you need to read 200. It's a good way to get a perspective on how textiles fit into history and the history of trade.'

His eight books have given him credibility and helped him gain access to museums and their textile curators, who can help answer questions he has and vice versa. 'It works both ways,' he says, citing an example where he provided information to the Victoria and Albert Museum on the different castes in Gujarat. The knowledge he had acquired directly from the people was otherwise not available. His contribution, he says, is to introduce textiles that may not have been seen before, because he goes to places that most others never visit.

'What you have to remember is that in this business we're all addicts. That includes many of our best customers. If I see a good textile and I can afford it, I'll buy it. This whole house is full of textiles. I go to my bed through two big piles of textiles.'

1 https://www.broadlandmemories.co.uk/blog/2011/06/from-barsham-to-albion-the-east-anglian-fairs/
2 Baluchi – from Baluchistan, a Pakistani province in the southwest, adjacent to Sindh. A charpoy is a cot made of woven rope.

above
Dida cloak or dance-robe made up of pieces from old plaited and tie-died raffia skirts, Côte d'Ivoire

opposite
Indigo-dyed *adire* eleko cloth from the 1960s in the Ibadan Dun pattern, Nigeria

Riders to Kabul

'I was walking from village to village in Swat, in a remote area with no roads bordering the tribal areas in Pakistan. I was looking for carved wood doors and windows to buy,' says Andy Hale. It was the 1980s and he had begun to sell architectural elements from the region, among other things, in the shop he and his wife, Kate Fitz Gibbon,¹ had opened in Santa Fe, New Mexico. They had previously worked in Afghanistan since the early 1970s.

'An old man with a long beard approached me in the village of Bahrain and asked, "Is this foreigner interested in buying our mosque?" He told me one and a half lakh rupees for the whole thing. I said OK without even seeing all the rooms inside. I just shook the guy's hand, turned to my translator and said, 'Did I just buy a mosque?''

opener
Detail of an ikat hanging, Uzbekistan, 1850–1875. National Museum of Asian Art, S2004.70, Gift of Guido Goldman

above
Andy Hale buying kilims from Uzbek traders in Afghanistan, circa 1975

opposite
Detail of an ikat hanging, Uzbekistan, 19th century. The Textile Museum, 2015.11.29, Gift of Guido Goldman in honor of Bruce P. Baganz

It is a long way from Berkeley, California, where both Hale and Fitz Gibbon are from, to the remote border region of Afghanistan and Pakistan; yet Hale's presence there wasn't surprising. He and Fitz Gibbon are children of the sixties from Berkeley, California, where there was at the time a lot of interest in this part of the world. On the hippie scene, it was associated with Eastern mysticism, drugs and colourful attire and objects, including rugs.

Hale bought his first Afghan rug, already his favourite type, when he was sixteen, when he and a friend visited an auction at Berkeley's Claremont Hotel. In 1972, after studying art in college for a year, the nineteen-year-old Hale decided he knew enough to go to Afghanistan to buy carpets. He had gone to rug shows, talked to rug dealers and read rug books so, in his mind, he already knew all about them.

Hale's exuberant belief in his expertise was premature, as he soon realised, but eventually it would become true. After decades of living through turbulence and turmoil in Afghanistan, and travelling widely in the region collecting, researching, producing and selling carpets, textiles and other local materials, Hale and Fitz Gibbon did, in fact, become world-renowned authorities on the material culture of Central Asia. Together they authored the catalogue for an exhibition of the antique ikat collection of London dealer Pip Rau,² and wrote an award-winning book on the ikat collection of the academic and philanthropist Guido Goldman.³

above
The town of Tashkurgan in northern
Afghanistan, 1970
opposite
Andy Hale in an antiques shop in
Afghanistan, 1970s

Their book on Uzbek embroidery helped introduce the little-known material to the West.[4]

Back in 1972, propelled by his curiosity and determination to buy carpets, Hale took his chances and flew to London where, at the time, you could find a place to stay for five pounds a night. Rumours that there was a bus from London to Kathmandu, Nepal for a mere £50 ($125) made it seem eminently possible to get to Afghanistan, a stop on the hippie trail across Asia.

Hale was staying in Earl's Court in London – known as Kangaroo Court in those days because it was popular with Australians – looking for a cheap way to get to Kabul, because there were no hippie buses leaving any time soon. In keeping with the anything-is-possible zeitgeist, Hale walked out of the hotel and saw a young Pakistani man standing by a Volkswagen bus with a sign saying 'riders to Kabul'. Hale just walked up to him and said he was going to Kabul. 'He thought I was joking,' Hale says.

The ride turned out to have more benefits than just getting Hale from here to there. The driver was Shi'i Muslim and part of his family was from Afghanistan, so he spoke Persian as well as Urdu and Punjabi.[5] During the weeks of travelling in that bus, Hale was able to learn some Afghan Persian, known as Dari, which came in handy once he reached Kabul where it was spoken. His reasons for the trip couldn't have been more different from those of the bus owner. 'I was going to see carpets, and Sufis and make some money to go back to university,' Hale says, but the twenty-something VW owner, who had lived in London since he was a teenager, was reluctantly returning to Kabul, at his parents' insistence, to marry a bride they had chosen for him. Hale

was excited to be starting a much-anticipated new adventure, while his driver felt that his own life was at an end.

'He didn't want to get married but he felt he had no choice,' Hale says, adding that, 'Being a Westerner, it's all about you and what you want.' The idea that you would sacrifice the remotest thing for your family seemed very strange to Hale at that age. He encountered more things that were unfamiliar to him as he travelled further into the Islamic world. It was the holy month of Ramadan when they got to Turkey, and Hale's first experience in an Islamic country, with the Ramadan fasting ritual from sunrise to sunset.

The beautiful, newly built roads in Iran, after the bad ones in Turkey, were welcome, since the point was to get to Kabul as quickly as possible. Afghanistan was rarely accessible to foreigners until the late 1960s because, among other reasons, it didn't have adequate roads. By the time Hale arrived in 1972, the US and the Soviets had each built half of an almost complete ring road joining the main cities of Afghanistan, making the drive from Herat to Kabul very smooth.

When they crossed the border into Afghanistan, Hale found the people friendly and welcoming. At the time, he was unaware that Afghans were obliged, according to a cultural custom of hospitality called *mehman nawazi*, to feed, protect and care for a guest. He later saw how deeply rooted the custom was when he asked for directions: instead of being told the way, he would be taken by the arm and walked to his destination, even though it was a mile away.

The cultures he met with had surprising similarities to the ethos of the hippies pouring into the country. 'To a long-haired Pashtun truck driver who smoked hash, whose truck was painted with brightly coloured movie actors and local scenery, a bunch of hippies showing up in their painted Volkswagen buses, guys with long hair who wanted to smoke hash, wasn't much of a culture clash.'

Kabul was a lively blend of Uzbeks, Pashtuns, Tajiks, Hazaras and Turkmens. Many wore traditional clothes that identified them by ethnic group or region. There were colourful flowing robes, assorted headgear from pakol[6] to bright embroidered caps and turbans, and some had orange-hennaed beards. The daily novelty of the bazaar was intoxicating for Hale.

Although it was the search for carpets that had prompted Hale to go to Afghanistan, what first caught his eye in the Kabul bazaar were Lakai and Kungrat embroideries, something he had never seen before. The people of various Uzbek tribes who live in northern Afghanistan came to Kabul to sell many of their precious belongings. A recent famine accounted for the plentiful supply of their exceptional embroidery in the market at that time. Hale was mesmerised by the small embroideries made for personal use by various tribes and would later explore them extensively with Fitz Gibbon while researching their book about Uzbek embroidery.

Back in Berkeley after his month in Afghanistan, Hale told Fitz Gibbon, who was then a university student, that they should move there. In the summer of 1973 they headed back to Europe and took trains and buses overland to Kabul. This time it was ikat, a resist-dyed textile, that caught Hale's eye, and he began to collect them. Later, he and and Fitz Gibbon would make major contributions to ikat studies.

Young and romantic, Hale told Fitz Gibbon he could imagine spending his whole life in Afghanistan. An experienced old Asia hand he knew advised him not to even say such a thing, warning him, 'There could be a coup tomorrow.' Two days later, on 18 July 1973, King Mohammed Zahir Shah was overthrown by his cousin Daoud Khan, who became president and changed the country from a monarchy to a republic. 'It a was fairly uneventful coup,' Hale recalls, 'but there was some shooting from airplanes.' Since no visas were being renewed at that time, the couple went to Pakistan and India, collecting Tibetan objects, and eventually headed home with various items they had bought. Hale describes it as 'probably a lot of junk, because we hadn't yet developed a sense of what was rare'.

Hale went back to art school, but after one term he realised that travel had seeped into his blood. He returned to Kabul in 1975 and took up full-time residence in the Cavaliers Hotel. From there, he started to make regular trips around the country and came to better understand its complexities. Afghanistan had a reputation as a 'simple' place, where you quickly feel you're fitting in, but Hale sensed he hadn't understood much at all. 'You can think that you're speaking really good Persian because people are very polite and no one will ever correct you,' he says, but when he started to refer to books and take language lessons he discovered his grammar was 'absolutely wonky'.

The one year he had planned to live in Kabul stretched into three. Fitz Gibbon was going back and forth. She had become a restorer of antique carpets and was working, between trips to Kabul, for Murray Eiland, widely considered an authority on antique rugs, in his shop in Berkeley.

In Kabul, Hale was learning how to find the best deals. Like other foreigners, he went to shops in Shar-e-Naw,[7] where the dealers spoke English, but they often held their best textiles for certain customers. As his Persian improved, he could bypass the shops and trade directly with people who came in from the countryside to sell carpets, who would walk the streets every morning with whatever they were selling. 'If they had something I wanted, I would make them an offer. They would sell it to me for less than the shopkeepers, because I paid cash on the spot instead of a bit each month, as the shopkeepers did, which meant they didn't have to come to Kabul so often.' A lot of the traders he met on the street were people who collected things from surrounding villages and took them to Kabul to sell. Hale used the opportunity to learn as much as he could from them about where everything was from, who made it and what it was called.

Around this time a book of new textile research came out, David and Thomas Knorr Lindahl's *Uzbek*,[8] greatly enhancing Hale's knowledge of what he had been buying and why it was now available in Afghanistan. The situation is explained succinctly in Hale and Fitz Gibbon's own book, *Ikat: Splendid Silks of Central Asia*, published in 1999.

The Bolshevik Revolution in Central Asia sent thousands of refugees across the southern border to Afghanistan [in the 1920s], and the emigres carried robes and wall-hangings with them when they fled. The textiles remained within families until necessity and Western demand forced them on to the market. Initially, ikats and embroidered textiles were brought to the West as a complement to the trade in Asian tribal rugs. In comparison to carpets, there were only very limited quantities of antique ikats available in either East or West, and a few knowing collectors quickly dominated the market.[9]

Afghanistan had long been closed to outsiders. Now that there were foreigners with money, things stored long ago began to come out of their boxes. Few in the West knew about Lakai or Kungrat embroideries, Uzbek suzanis or ikat from the 19th-century Central Asian khanates, Hale says, until he and others started collecting and importing them. There was an abundant supply available in excellent condition. 'People would take textiles out for a wedding or to decorate a honeymoon room, but they didn't keep them hanging on a wall.'

Hale wasn't the biggest dealer in Kabul so he needed to find a way to get a jump on the others. In 1976 some of the dealers he had met on the Kabul streets – among them Abdul Rauf and Ghulam Siddiq – invited him to buy directly from them in Tashkurgan, an ancient town in the Balkh province of northern Afghanistan, where they lived. 'They didn't like Kabul – it was a big city and they had to stay in a hotel,' Hale says. It worked well for all if he travelled to them instead. Knowing the language meant Hale could also understand the culture and he was soon 'adopted' by the '*qaum*' of the traders he was working with. *Qaum* means community – people on whom you depend and who depend on you.

Hale established a monthly routine collecting carpets and textiles from towns and villages outside Kabul, becoming familiar with the different communities each place he went. 'Aqcha was fascinating because it was Turkmen. Tashkurgan was mostly Persian-speaking – although there were also Turkmens and Arabs living nearby.' Hale would throw a bunch of cash in a little backpack and take a bus or shared taxi which let him out by the side of the road. From there he would get on a horse cart – there were no cars then in the town– and they would take him into Tashkurgan, which still resembled a caravan city of earlier years. A ruined mud-brick castle several centuries old loomed over the town.

'I'd spend the night there and my friends would send food over to the hotel. I'd get up early in the morning and hit the beautiful old bazaar. It was a place of traditional crafts, small open-fronted shops and inviting *chai-khanas* [teahouses]. You could sit on a mud-brick *takht*, a bench, by the side of the street, sipping tea while puffing on a hookah, and watch life pass by. I knew a number of the people there and I was able to buy very nice things. If I bought a lot, I'd just leave it there and they would bring it to Kabul for me.'

He would move on to Mazar-i-Sharif, Balkh and Aqcha, arriving at the same time each month. People were expecting him. 'They would collect things they had from the old days for me because, with our new knowledge, suddenly they were worth something.'

Once a large and prosperous city of mud brick some three square miles in area, Balkh was surrounded by walls pierced by seven gates. A Friday mosque occupied the centre, and many more mosques were scattered among the dwellings. The city was once home to not only Persians and Turkic peoples but also communities of Jews and Indian traders, poets and scholars, lawyers, geographers and astronomers. Catastrophe struck in 1220, when raids by 100,000 Mongol horsemen left nothing standing. Balkh remained in ruins for a century until Timur (Tamerlane) chose Balkh to proclaim his accession to the throne (1359) and restored the walls and endowed the city with splendid buildings, some of which survive. Mazar-i-Sharif ('Tomb of the Exalted') rose to prominence

opposite
Detail of a Lakai embroidery, Uzbekistan, 19th century. Minneapolis Institute of Art, 2004.259.82, Gift of Jack A. and Aviva Robinson

more recently, in the 19th century. It is home to Uzbeks, Tajiks, Hazaras and Pashtuns, and a centre for trade in Karakol lambskins and carpets. The city is named after and known for the shrine of Sharif Ali.[10]

Hale and Fitz Gibbon were also working with Turkmen weavers to make new carpets. Turkmen men would come in winter from Baba Sadiq (177 miles northwest of Kabul) to Tashkurgan, where Hale would show them the weaving-design graph. The subject of price would have to wait until the next day until the women, who wove the rugs, could look at the design. A certain propriety meant Hale never met the women. Fitz Gibbon could spend time with and photograph them, however, capturing their unique style of dress and distinctive silver jewellery.

Hale had to find additional ways to make money because, at that time, there wasn't much to be made in selling textiles or carpets. He stuck his finger, literally, into many different pots – reviving natural dyeing, having Hazara women weave sweaters, clearing things through customs for Mir Ayaz, an Uzbek carpet dealer in Kabul. 'I was very close to him,' says Hale, explaining that Mir Ayaz was too busy to spend all day at the airport, so Hale would do the administration for him. Clearing customs was complicated. If there was cotton in the carpets you had to negotiate, because only wool was allowed, and they had to be baled a certain way. 'I was living off the kickbacks – 10 per cent from the freight bill.'

In 1977 Hale went back to Berkeley for a month but he felt alienated there. He had become acculturated to Kabul – America seemed a very strange place to him. Back in Kabul, he continued his monthly journeys to the north and his life seemed to be following a steady path. One day in spring 1978, however, he was in the midst of a conversation with a friend on the street when they heard loud banging. At first dismissing it as noise from a construction site, they soon realised it was a machine gun and rushed into a shop to ask what was happening. 'Enkalab', they were told – 'revolution'. A communist coup had begun.

Hale was not in danger to begin with, but by late 1978 'all hell had broken loose'. Communists were killing communists. The Mujahideen were resisting the communists.[11] Nobody knew from day to day if they were going to live or die. After the American ambassador, Adolph Dubs, was kidnapped and murdered in a botched rescue attempt in 1979, there was no safety no matter who you were.[12]

Despite the chaos, and although friends and family were urging him to return home, Hale didn't want to leave. 'It was one of those situations where you think that things are so bad it can't get worse,' he says, but in fact it did. You could hear shooting every night. He knew people who were being taken away and tortured, and some people just disappeared. Many Afghans started emigrating to Germany or Pakistan.

Hale doesn't believe he, or his Peace Corps housemates, who were soon called back to the US, were very high on the communists' enemies list, but he was concerned for their cook and gardener when he learned their house was being watched. 'They wouldn't take foreigners in for interrogation, but they would take your servants and beat the hell out of them and make them talk about whatever you were doing.' Uzbek friends, who had been pleased to see him studying their language, told him never to speak it because they didn't want anyone to think they were communicating in a secret language. With great sadness he closed his house in Kabul in 1980 and returned to the US. After that, he would fly in, check into a hotel for a month or two, buy a bunch of stuff and go back to the US.

In the 1980s, Hale says, it was very hard to work in Kabul. Just staying warm and finding food took a lot of time, so most of the dealers and shopkeepers in his community left the country, moving across the border to Peshawar in Pakistan.

Hale took an apartment in Peshawar and would go there for a month at a time. He actually had greater access there to different people – Turkmen, Uzbek, Pashtun and Tajik, from all over Afghanistan – because they were all in one place. 'I saw them all day every day, since they had nothing to do but talk to you.' There were entire bazaars with nothing but Afghan goods. One was in a five-storey building hosting a beehive of tiny shops selling carpets, textiles, jewellery, beadwork and handmade glass items from Herat.

In between trips to Peshawar, Hale was spending his time in Los Angeles, where he and Fitz Gibbon had moved, because more money and more collectors were there compared with the Bay Area. At first they would drive around to see collectors, toting a couple of big suitcases, selling all kinds of things they had bought in Afghanistan – antiques, literally tons of jewellery – but few textiles. 'We had bought a lot of textiles but we deliberately kept them for ourselves.' Soon, they were importing whole containers of goods and selling wholesale at gift shows around the country.

1986 was a turning point. Pip Rau asked Hale and Fitz Gibbon to write the text for the catalogue of an exhibition, organised by the London Crafts Council, of the Central Asian ikats she had collected. They had met Rau in the 1970s in Kabul, where Hale had introduced her to Abdul Rauf, one

Photo: Anita Herle

above
Street scene in Kandahar, southern
Afghanistan, 1970s
opposite
Men cooking at a wedding in
Tashkurgan, northern Afghanistan,
1970s

of his main suppliers who also became one of hers. They agreed to write the catalogue, thinking they could bang it out in an afternoon or two.

It was their first foray into writing and a lot more work than they anticipated. 'We did archival research, found good sources and did some translation,' says Hale. Although the experience took much longer and was more complex than they had expected, the catalogue opened a lot of doors for them.

'We were able to write an article on Lakai[13] for HALI – "The bad beys of Central Asia" – using, for the first time, Soviet sources for an English publication on Lakai textiles.' They had been told that there was no point doing research because everything written in Russian had already been translated and assimilated. Their fieldwork, however, gave them the distinct advantage of talking to people on the ground who revealed that only a tiny fraction of what's in the archives had actually been translated into English.

The fall of the Soviet Union in 1991 meant that archives in Uzbekistan became accessible for the first time to outsiders. These resources included the Navoi Library, the records of museums in Tashkent and Samarkand and sources drawing on an archive dating back to the 18th century in Khiva. Until then, Hale was 'scared to death' of Uzbekistan. 'I remember being in Baba Sadiq (Afghanistan) in the late 1970s and looking across the border. It was like looking at a prison. Just chilling.'[14]

By 1995 Hale and Fitz Gibbon had moved to Santa Fe, New Mexico, and opened a big shop where they sold old copper, metal and ironwork, carved wooden doors and textiles. 'You could buy and export old suzanis from Central Asia after the fall of the Soviet Union so I was buying fifty-year-old examples and other things, like jewellery, that people made for themselves, not for tourists, that were affordable,' he says.

By the early 2000s the climate in Pakistan had become radicalised. Hale finally gave up going there after witnessing a huge demonstration in Qissa Khwani, one of the main bazaars in Peshawar, where people were cursing Jews and shouting 'Death to Americans!' 'Everyone knew me,' he says. 'They said "We don't mean you, Andy," but it wasn't a good situation.'

To avoid the constant kidnappings, bombings and growing tension in Pakistan, Hale started buying in Turkey, which was being flooded with goods from Central Asia after the fall of the USSR. 'Every little region in Central Asia has their own stuff,' he points out. 'You would see a whole lot of one kind of rug or embroidery for around six months and then it would be gone.'

By the mid 1990s, Hale was 'burned out' on the textile scene. 'There were very few serious textile collectors, and some weren't that easy to work with,' he says. One however, Guido Goldman,[15] became 'a very big thing in our lives'. Goldman had previously bought many rare ikats from them through his New York dealer, Gail Martin, but they had never met him.

After collecting ikats for twenty years Goldman decided to exhibit what had arguably become the best such collection in the world. He asked Hale and Fitz Gibbon to write the definitive book on Central Asian ikats and the catalogue that would accompany seven exhibitions, which would feature many of the hundreds of ikats in his collection. The first of these, mounted in 1997 at the Museum of Fine Arts in Boston, was only the second time that an American museum had organised a major show of Central Asian ikats.

Realising the wide scope of the book, Hale proposed to undertake research in Uzbekistan and Russian archives and museums where there were photographs and documentary material that had been collected by expeditions within Central Asia. 'The textiles often have records of provenance and you can see who made it, where and when it was collected,' Hale says. Although such research would be expensive, Goldman agreed it was important to do and gave them carte blanche to go anywhere they needed. 'Guido was a dream date for research. How rare is it that two people are told that, whatever you need, just go and do it?'

Suzuki Kaku / Alamy Stock Photo

above
Terraced fields in the Swat Valley of Pakistan

Hale and Fitz Gibbon threw themselves into the research, travelling to St Petersburg, Moscow, Tashkent, Bukhara and Samarkand where they visited museums, combed the archives and met with academics, curators, authors and experts. 'We went from museum to museum asking to see their collections,' Hale says. 'We wanted to see pieces that had been collected "scientifically", that had documentation, or that had been collected by expeditions. Every piece had an index card, called a passport, with information.' They found pictures that had never been published in the West. 'We made copies of photographs of craft production that were some of the earliest survey photos taken in Central Asia in the 1860s.'

The project was a massive undertaking. Specialist Russian dictionaries were required for old technical terms; photographers spent months getting the right pictures; dye experts conducted analysis; and special boxes had to be manufactured for the oversize volume. 'We and others were working twenty-four hours a day around the world in Russia, Uzbekistan, the UK and the US for a full two years.'

The scholarly book exposed ikat to a world in the US and Europe far beyond the small group of textile collectors already familiar with it. 'You just didn't see that many great ikats in quantity until Guido's book,' Hale says. 'All of a sudden, everyone wanted ikat.'

Referring to the fact that Goldman insisted his collection be shown as art, not craft, Hale stipulates that 'Ikat isn't an ethnic craft made by just Uzbeks or Turkmen. It was made by all kinds of people – Persian speakers, Jews – so it was a commercial art dependant on novelty and innovation. There was no fixed tradition in its design. It has a Central Asian aesthetic but it doesn't have the character of an ethnic art.'

Unexpectedly, the book was also instrumental in the revival of traditional ikat production in Uzbekistan. One of their Uzbek colleagues showed the photos to the old weavers who had kept ikat alive, to some extent, during the Soviet era when private production was forbidden. Spurred by increasing demand for 'antique' ikats – first for haute couture fashion and then for a far wider audience – ikat workshops began to proliferate. A true renewal of the art resulted: 'It's unbelievable what they did in such a short time,' Hale says.

Hale and Fitz Gibbon also loved Uzbek nomadic embroidery and wanted to do a book about it. Little international exposure had been given to the stunning textiles created for local use, such as interior fabrics, dowry treasures, and items defining social and cultural identity. In 2005 they got the chance when they were asked to write a catalogue for an exhibition of the Jack and Aviva Robinson Collection at the Minneapolis Institute of Art. 'We were blessed because the Robinsons, like Goldman, understood that it takes time and money to go out and do real research,' Hale says, adding that there are numerous books on Central Asian textiles by people who have spent little or no time in Central Asia.

Hale's and Fitz Gibbon's working method was unlike the way most people do textile books. 'We work collaboratively with the local people. We visit people in the field who are also studying and, in some cases, we include contributions by them.' Getting information was complicated by the issue of 'shirk', which means superstition or idolatry, making symbolism and meaning a touchy subject. 'It's a very personal thing,' Hale acknowledges. Finding ways to learn first-hand about the embroidery was tricky since, for decades, anthropology as a scholarly study had been curtailed in the Soviet Union. Much in traditional Muslim culture was denigrated – said to be based on the remains of pre-Islamic, shamanist culture. 'All questions about the organisation of society had been determined by Lenin and Stalin so there was no apparent need for anthropology,' even though Uzbek embroidery is honoured within the entire social structure.

The Uzbek people of Central Asia consider skilful embroidery an indicator of personal industry and refinement. Particular emphasis is placed on artistic accomplishment as well as technical excellence. Their embroideries not only bring status to the community and honour to the household, but they also function as vehicles of cultural memory and continuity. Their colourful embroideries explore the balance between traditional parameters and the aesthetic freedom of individual artists.

One of the first post-Soviet Central Asian anthropologists, Binafsha Nodir, who was Kungrat, worked in partnership with them to collect information, including from women embroiderers within her own community. Meanwhile Hale and Fitz Gibbon conducted archival research of photographs from expeditions dating back to the 1920s, met with experts, and visited the Lakai in Tajikistan.

Looking back, Hale reflects on the impact of carpet and textile collectors systematically removing every good example from where they originated. 'I had to bring fragments of old Turkmen carpets to Turkmen people who were trying to revive their carpet traditions – because they had never seen a 19th-century carpet,' he says. This lack of historic models in the locality means that newer carpets are not as good as the older ones. Hale nevertheless admonishes 'smug' collectors who won't look at anything made within the past eighty years, those who 'think they know more about the carpet than the woman who wove it.'

opposite

Lakai embroidery, Uzbekistan, 19th century. Minneapolis Institute of Art, 2004.259.83, Gift of Jack A. and Aviva Robinson

Talking of the relocation of artefacts, whatever happened to that impulse buy of a mosque in the Swat Valley? And why was it for sale? The villagers explained to Hale that at every election the politicians had promised to build a school for local children. 'That's what we want,' he was told, 'but they never build it. This is the only thing in our community that we can sell to build a school with.' Hale says: 'It was a traditional mosque made of stone and mudbrick, with carved wood pillars, doors and panels with plain stucco walls. I paid them, agreeing that it was better to have a school for their children than to have a bunch of old stuff sitting around.' He negotiated a price to dismantle and move the pieces 1,000 miles from the village to the seaport of Karachi.

When he returned to the village six months later, the people in the village still hadn't moved the mosque but, he noted, 'They sure enough had built a school. There were girls on the right and boys on the left with their little boards and chalk and they were learning the alphabet and how to read. Even though they're very religious people,' he adds 'they don't worship the *stuff*. There was nothing sacred about the wood of the mosque itself.' The doors were incredible, Hale says, and even though he owned them he gave them back to the village.

Looking forward, he hopes to see objects going back to Central Asia where they will be appreciated and understood on Central Asian terms. On a recent trip to Uzbekistan, he was impressed with the younger generation, who are now allowed to study historical and cultural subjects that were previously forbidden. Thirty-five new books on cultural heritage have been published in Uzbekistan by the World Society for the Study, Preservation, and Popularization of the Cultural Legacy of Uzbekistan.

When he started, Hale recounts, 'It was me going into the bazaar, negotiating with Uzbeks, trying to understand their culture, driving around the US with suitcases and going into people's houses to see their collections.' That has changed dramatically over the past twenty years, he says, and now 'it's all done online. This was a world I never could have imagined when I was on the steppes of Central Asia and everything was very personal and intimate. Even in the nineties, I couldn't imagine that anyone would buy a carpet or textile online.'

'There's nothing new about Westerners going to Asia and buying beautiful things. It goes back to Marco Polo. But I think we're the last generation. When I went to Kabul, it was the only place where you could see all this material. Now, with the internet, why would anybody go to Kabul?'

1 See Kate Fitz Gibbon, p. 166.

2 Kate Fitz Gibbon and Andrew Hale, *Ikats: Woven Silks from Central Asia: The Rau Collection*. Basil Blackwell in cooperation with the Crafts Council, 1988.

3 Kate Fitz Gibbon and Andrew Hale, *IKAT: Silks of Central Asia, The Guido Goldman Collection*, Laurence King Publishing, 1997, was the winner of the George Wittenborn Memorial Award for Best Art Book of 1997.

4 Kate Fitz Gibbon and Andrew Hale, *Uzbek Embroidery in the Nomadic Tradition*, Minneapolis Institute of Art, 2007.

5 Afghan Dari is one of the Persian languages spoken in Afghanistan. Urdu and Punjabi are two of the languages spoken in Pakistan.

6 A soft, round-topped wool hat for men, found in earthy colours.

7 *Shar-e-Naw* means new city; it is the name of a neighbourhood in Kabul.

8 David and Thomas Knorr Lindahl, *Uzbek: The Textiles and Life of the Nomadic and Sedentary Uzbek Tribes of Central Asia*, Zbinden Druck und Verlag AG, 1975.

9 *Ikat: Splendid Silks of Central Asia*, Hale and Fitz Gibbon, p. 16.

10 https://depts.washington.edu/silkroad/cities/afghanistan/balkh.html

11 The Saur Revolution (April Revolution or April Coup), was led by the Soviet-backed People's Democratic Party of Afghanistan (PDPA) against the rule of Afghan President Mohammed Daoud Khan on 27–28 April 1978. Daoud Khan and most of his family were killed. The revolution was the precursor to the 1979 intervention by the Soviets and the 1979–1989 Soviet-Afghan war against the Mujahideen, loosely aligned Afghan opposition groups who rebelled against the government of the pro-Soviet Democratic Republic of Afghanistan (DRA).

12 'Forty-two years on, the precise circumstances surrounding the death of the 58-year-old diplomat remain shrouded in mystery. Several questions remain unanswered, including who was behind Dubs' kidnapping, who fired the fatal shots, and whether the Soviet Union was involved.' https://www.rferl.org/a/years-on-mystery-still-surrounds-shooting-death-of-u-s-ambassador-to-afghanistan/29770272.html

13 The Lakai are an Uzbek tribe of the Dasht-i-Kipchak steppe peoples in Central Asia.

14 After Uzbekistan declared independence from the Soviet Union in 1991, Islam Karimov was elected as the first president of Uzbekistan. He remained in power, after a series of elections not recognised by most international observers, until he died in 2016.

15 Goldman's family came to the US after being forced to flee Germany. A Harvard graduate and then professor, he replaced Henry Kissinger as director of Harvard's Minda de Gunzburg Center for European Studies. He is especially known for his work to build positive relations between Germany and the United States, among these, his founding of the German Marshall Fund of the United States.

opposite

Detail of a velvet ikat hanging, Uzbekistan, circa 1850–1875. The Textile Museum, 2015.11.98, Gift of Guido Goldman in honor of Bruce P. Baganz

Kate Fitz Gibbon

Seeing every piece in the bazaar

'I was nineteen. I didn't even know where Afghanistan was. But I was very close friends with Andy [Hale] and he was about to go someplace that was 12,000 miles away and had no phone service. He wanted to start a business with textiles there. I gave him my college money. Then I followed the money. My impulse was purely to follow a friend, who I've ended up being married to for the past forty-five years.'

Kate Fitz Gibbon was curious, adventurous and willing to explore. Raised in an artistic household she appreciated textiles and art, but what interested her most in Afghanistan were the people and the culture. 'It wasn't the things, it was the place, their way of life, their relationships to each other. I was so clearly an outsider, so obviously knew nothing about them. A little bit babe in the woods, helpless, because I had no idea how to function in that culture, but eager to try.'

Fitz Gibbon would spend the next thirty years absorbing everything she could about Central Asian culture, learning both in the region and at home in the US where, between trips to Afghanistan and Pakistan, she repaired carpets, became a dealer, opened a shop, studied Chinese, Persian and Russian, and authored books on Central Asian textiles.

opener
Detail of a Lakai embroidery, Uzbekistan, 19th–20th century. Minneapolis Institute of Art, 2004.259.61, Gift of Jack A. and Aviva Robinson
above
Kate Fitz Gibbon with a shipment of Afghan socks in the early 1980s, all marked 'large' regardless of size
opposite
Carpet market in Kizil Ayak, Afghanistan, 1978

She was appointed to the Cultural Property Advisory Committee by US President Bill Clinton in 2000 and was so disturbed by State Department missteps in policy and failure to follow the law that she became a lawyer, wrote on art law,[1] and took on another career. She's now the editor of the online *Cultural Property News*[2] and executive director of the non-profit Committee for Cultural Policy. No longer a 'babe in the woods', Fitz Gibbon became a major voice for heritage preservation and global access to culture.

When she arrived in Afghanistan with Hale in 1973, she fell in love with the country immediately. 'I knew at once that this was a place that was so different from what I had known.' Eighteenth-, 19th- and 20th-century textiles from Central Asia were the most beautiful in the world, says Fitz Gibbon, thanks to their artistic quality. That so little was known about them was a compelling reason for her to become a student of them. The best way to study the material, she thought, 'was to see every piece in the bazaar and have thousands of pieces flow through your hands'.

The priority was for her, as it was for Hale, to do whatever was needed to continue working in Afghanistan – which meant having a business with someone buying things there and someone selling things in the US.

above
Kate Fitz Gibbon in Delhi airport in 1988, awaiting the departure of a flight delayed three days by the shelling of Kabul airport by the Afghan resistance
opposite
Turkmen wedding in northern Afghanistan, 1973

Roland and Sabrina Michaud / akg-images

Hale moved to Afghanistan and Fitz Gibbon went back to Berkeley where, between studying at the University of California, she worked as a restorer for carpet dealer Murray Eiland, 'learning carpets from the inside out'. She and Andy consigned carpets to Eiland 'although he had little interest in the obscure, furry tribal textiles we liked best', and sold ikats and embroideries at flea markets on weekends. 'Gradually, we built connections to clients who had similar tastes, and many became friends.'

Hale and Fitz Gibbon took a chance on importing goods from a country most Americans had hardly heard of at the time. But they knew that many young people, like them, were seeking an alternative way of seeing the world, whether it was through mysticism, hashish or working in the Peace Corps. Archaeologists, anthropologists and other academics were travelling around the world exploring unknown cultures in a way that hadn't really happened since the 19th century. The Beatles were going to Manali and Dharamsala to meet with yogis, and dressing up in Indian clothing. All this was happening at the same time as the hippie movement was setting out to see the world.

Most of the people who were interested in Hale and Fitz Gibbon's carpets and textiles, not surprisingly, were young. Occasionally, a celebrity would come by. 'I remember Kareem Abdul-Jabbar ducking down a full two feet in order to get into Murray's store to buy a good, big Uzbek chapan – they make them big.[3] Initially, Fitz Gibbon's knowledge of what she was selling was minimal, but most buyers were interested only in the aesthetics. Because she and Andy bought all over Afghanistan, not just in Kabul, she could tell them where something came from, she says, 'but it took years for me to really know what I had'.

Whenever she could, Fitz Gibbon would fly back to Kabul to join Hale, usually staying for three months at a time before her visa would expire. She went with him up north to Tashkurgan, Aqcha, Balkh and Mazar-i-Sharif to talk to the people who had a more intimate knowledge of who made what, when and how. 'That was very much part of what we were interested in. We weren't there just to buy things. We've never been great at making money but we've always been good at research,' she says.

Travelling outside Kabul meant they were invited to family events, like weddings, in the towns and villages they visited. They saw first-hand how people lived and how they used the textiles they made.

At one of the weddings they attended, the men had constructed roofed pavilions out of kilims and carpets in a big space outside the house, and decorated the area, inside and out, with pillows. There was a dais on which a group of young men were singing and playing instruments. 'When we came in they started an extempore song about all the foreigners who were visiting Afghanistan and how wonderful it was, and welcoming us. Afghans are very good at improvised performance and poetry.'

As a female outsider, Fitz Gibbon could both sit with the men and gain insight into the daily lives of the women, although this came with its own cost. At family celebrations, like a wedding, she would eat first with the men, who did the cooking for the big feasts. 'The men outside, who had giant copper bowls over a fire, were making pilau. You have to eat a lot because it's polite,' she says. Then she was called to see the women inside the house where she would have to have another feast and eat just as much as she did with the men. 'There would be dozens and dozens of little girls wearing mascara and makeup and beautiful little dresses. Their more soberly dressed mothers and grandmothers were eating and chatting and shooing the children about. Others were singing, playing tambourines and dancing.'

Fitz Gibbon was welcomed into the private space of the women, but that didn't mean they knew what to make of her. 'Honestly, they thought I was really odd, but they were accepting,' she says, adding that she, too, had to adapt to their behaviour. 'There's a polite way of interacting – of deference and being respectful to elders.' Since multiple generations of families lived in a compound, it could be puzzling to figure out relationships. First-cousin marriages were considered the most appropriate, and often siblings in one family would be married to their cousins in another.

Before the Russians occupied the country in 1979, Hale and Fitz Gibbon regularly visited the homes of the families of their dealers in Tashkurgan. She remembers one occasion, in particular, when she climbed up the stairs into the reception area for women and passed rows of marijuana plants hanging upside down to dry in the stairway. 'That surprised me, but I didn't say anything.' She came to a room with carpets and felts on the floor and palettes placed around the edge. There she found half-a-dozen women doing embroidery and sipping tea. The little girls, who ran errands for the women, were bringing in baskets of sweets. As they were unloading them, Fitz Gibbon noticed one was full of worms. At first shocked 'and a little appalled', she then realised that they were silkworms eating mulberry leaves. 'This was just a bit of the household economy where they got the baskets mixed up,' she says.

opposite
Detail of an ikat hanging, Uzbekistan, circa 1800–1850. The Textile Museum, 2015.11.47, Gift of Guido Goldman in honor of Bruce P. Baganz

above
Gallery view of 'Binding the Clouds:
The Art of Central Asian Ikat',
comprising silk ikat panels and
hangings from the Guido Goldman
gift, on view at The Textile Museum
in Washington, DC, in 2018

The women Fitz Gibbon visited were as curious about her as she was about them. They wanted to feel her clothes, ask about schooling and the nature of her work. There was a loud exclamation of surprise when she explained that *she* kept the money they bought with, not Hale. When she said she didn't have children, she sensed it was a huge disappointment to them because they would have liked to exchange information about raising them. 'They were trying to find out what kinds of things I did that were like what they did. They wanted to know what was the same and what was different in my life compared to theirs.' Fitz Gibbon took many photographs and would bring them back copies. 'They were incredibly kind and generous to me. One young girl was so bright and sweet – and mischievous – that we named our first daughter after her, Malika. We've worried so much for all of them since we were cut off by the war.'

In all the years she spent in Afghanistan she had only two brief negative experiences – in Kabul and Kunduz – where someone was rude because she was a woman. In both cases, strangers nearby intervened, apologised, and told her that the person was mentally unwell. 'The Afghans had a dignity and a self-respect that translated into respect for others,' she says.

Once the Russians invaded, Fitz Gibbon and Hale had to break off relations with these Tashkurgan families, because to have European or American contacts threatened their safety and their lives. They also had to stop visiting the Chakir Turkmen people they were weaving carpets with, who lived within five miles of the Russian border. 'We were able to keep working with them but we weren't able to travel there. Nobody would believe we were just weaving carpets, would they?'

Their foray into making new carpets with the Turkmens was as much about having a reason to have more intimate contact with Turkmens as it was for the product. Forming a relationship, they believed, was the best way to find out what people do, how they work and worship, what they eat and wear. 'We needed a really good excuse to spend time in such a remote village – Baba Siddiq was hardly even a village, it was a group of families who had come over in the 1930s from what was then Uzbekistan into Afghanistan to escape collectivisation. We wanted to know all about them, so weaving the rugs was the excuse.' They would go up to the village and return at night to Tashkurgan, some ten miles away.

Hale found a Turkmen in the settlement who was willing to bring his family in on the weaving. A dyer in Tashkurgan, who was an elderly family member of one of the dealers they worked with, also committed to the project. Hale brought wool from Herat, in western Afghanistan, where the best wool was produced, and gave it to the dyers in Tashkurgan. 'We were buying natural dyes like indigo, trying to find properly aged madder where

above
Turkmen wedding in northern
Afghanistan, 1973
opposite
Painted truck in Kandahar,
Afghanistan, 1970s

the roots were three years old, and looking for the right mordants,' Fitz Gibbon says. She and Hale even did some of the natural dyeing themselves; she succeeded mainly in colouring her hands blue.

'We were intent on replicating the patterns and also the weave, heft and structure of earlier Turkmen carpets,' Fitz Gibbon says. Murray Eiland had initially done designs for very elaborate Beshir prayer carpets, which were quite different from the carpets traditionally woven by the Turkmen people they were working with. Hale and Fitz Gibbon also made some smaller designs based on Uzbek embroidered belts. All were graphed out knot-for-knot in colour on very large pieces of graph paper. 'The designs were extremely varied, even over-elaborate, with changing backgrounds.'

The women wove in yurts outside the mudbrick house. They did not speak any Persian so Fitz Gibbon used a lot of sign language. She took pictures with a Polaroid camera and gave them the photos as a gift. The women had small mirrors, Fitz Gibbon says, but they were so unused to seeing things in two dimensions that they did not initially recognise themselves, or each other, in the photos. When she showed them black-and-white photos in carpet books, they said that the carpets must have been in the sun too long and lost all their colour. 'They brought different eyes and a different mindset to this,' says Fitz Gibbon. But she had not yet grasped the full extent of those differences.

Three weeks after she gave them the paper designs, their contact in the village gave them back, saying the carpets would be ready in three months. When asked why they didn't want to keep the papers, he replied that they didn't need them. The couple took the designs back to Kabul with no expectations, thinking, God knows what will happen with this.

Three months later they saw the woven sample carpets. They were knot-for-knot exactly the same as the designs. The weavers pointed out that they had even corrected a 'mistake' they found in the pattern. Fitz Gibbon saw, once again, that the women weavers had a distinctive way of thinking about pattern or design and understood weaving on a level that was completely inaccessible to her. 'They not only memorised the design but they knew where it was wrong and fixed it. They were capable of filling in the blank without putting it on paper, just holding it in their mind. That just blew me away.'

Fitz Gibbon still has a couple of those carpets but, she says, they didn't make many of them; other people, like Hajji Muhammed Yusuf, who was a carpet restorer in Kabul, started to make carpets and knew much better how to do it. 'He knew perfectly well what we were doing and not just because I was walking around with blue hands. There are no secrets in Kabul,' Fitz Gibbon says. This was the beginning of the silk carpet weaving industry in Kabul and Hajji Muhammed Yusuf was one of the very first, if not the first. 'We knew him really well, he was practically a saint,' she says. The Hazara,[4] who are much discriminated against, had suffered more than others even in the early part of the war. There were many orphans and Yusuf and his wife, who had no children, took the children into their home and treated them like their own. They gave them jobs weaving rugs using natural dyes in wool and silk.

As they became more and more interested in textiles, Fitz Gibbon and Hale became aware of the weakness of the scholarship on textiles and carpets from the Uzbek, Aimaq, Arab and Kirgiz groups in Afghanistan. Soviet writers in the 1930s and 40s had written about carpets being made by various groups, but Americans tended to reject the work of Soviet scholars. Another gap in American scholarship was field research. 'No one seemed to feel that there was anything to be learned from talking to the people themselves. They might not have woven the 19th-century carpets but their grandmothers had, and they still retained pieces of these beautiful early rugs.'

The Turkmens Fitz Gibbon and Hale were making carpets with were very willing to show them scraps of old carpets they had kept, but they refused to sell them. They held onto them, they told Fitz Gibbon, 'because they're good to look at when you get old'. They appreciated their quality and that they were completely different from the commercial carpets they were weaving to order that were based on Western styles and tastes. 'They knew how to weave aesthetically pleasing, complex patterns and they were critical of the boring rugs the Kabul dealers commissioned,' says Fitz Gibbon. 'But people who were writing carpet books weren't particularly interested in what Turkmens thought about their own weavings.'

Hale and Fitz Gibbon began to give lectures on the research they'd done for their own interest and pleasure. 'What's more fun than learning about something? And what's more fun than learning about something that hasn't really been explored before?' They collected 19th- and early 20th-century books in Russian because Russian travellers such as Samuil Dudin had done significant field research;[5] other Russian sources discussed trade, dyeing, the distribution of ethnic groups and other information Fitz Gibbon and Hale passionately wanted to explore.

By the mid 1980s they were being recognised as experts on the textiles of Central Asia. The first book they wrote was a catalogue of the ikat collection of their friend and fellow dealer Pip Rau.[6] Their dream of being able to travel to do in-depth research came true when Dr Guido Goldman asked them to write a catalogue of his exceptional ikat collection. 'We had a patron totally committed to scholarship and the most wonderful collection in the world to work with – over 300 wall hangings and dozens of robes made of the earliest ikats, the ones that had the experimental design, vitality and jazzy musical quality of the very best early 19th-century examples.'

Goldman was the head of the Minda de Gunzburg Center for European Studies at Harvard. When he wanted something done, she says, his criteria were to do the research and do it right. With a Harvard library card in hand, she was able to access one of only two copies in US libraries of a book on the Lakai by Belkis Khalilovna Karmysheva, among many other hard-to-find publications. The first seventeen pages of Karmysheva's work had been excised with a razor blade because, between the time the author had written it and the time it was published, Stalin had died and she had thanked all the wrong people, Fitz Gibbon says.

The timing for the project couldn't have been better. After the fall of the Soviet Union in 1991, the Soviet archives were more accessible, and travel to former Soviet republics was easier. The couple used the opportunity to meet with academics, museologists

and other scholars in Moscow, St Petersburg, Tashkent, Bukhara, as well as London, Oxford and various American cities and museums. They threw themselves into the project conducting research on a subject that hadn't yet been covered in depth. Fitz Gibbon had started to study Russian privately when they began research for the Rau catalogue and continued while researching the Goldman book, but she was 'only a beginner'. They also hired a translator to deal with the volume of materials and ensure everything was correct. 'We had wonderful colleagues in Russia and Uzbekistan who helped us to find additional sources,' Fitz Gibbon says. Working in Uzbekistan, they found that textile authority Sayora Makhamova had used the catalogue they wrote for Pip Rau's exhibition to try to replicate 19th-century ikat designs and production in the Fergana Valley in Uzbekistan.

Their years of fieldwork, in addition to their own research studies, provided them with unique background knowledge of the culture and the broad context for the production of ikat in the 19th century, as witnessed by this extract from the Goldman book:

> During a hundred-year long cultural and economic revival in the oasis kingdoms, ikat dyeing became the most vital, sophisticated and widely distributed textile art in Central Asia... The nineteenth-century designers drew inspiration from many sources; in ikat the decorative traditions of urban embroidery and wall painting were combined with the dynamic energy of the steppe nomads. In essence the Central Asian ikats were a commercial art-form that transcended the limitations of the market-place. Their inventive pattern and explosive color needed no interpreter – ikats traveled across the steppes as booty, as trade goods, and as gifts of robes of honor from proud Khans to the great Tsar.[7]

Their books and articles on Central Asian textiles expanded a previously neglected field of study in the West. In the 1970s, Fitz Gibbon says, only a few books a year were published on Central Asia, if you could find them. For her, as a student at Berkeley who was interested in studying the region, only Iranian Persian was offered in the language department.[8] With the war in Afghanistan, Central Asia became a hot topic and, after glasnost, archives in Russia and Central Asia opened up. With greater access, many more scholars now worked in the region.

Others were also writing about Central Asian textiles, Fitz Gibbon says, but no one was doing the field research that they were taking on. That was the difference that distinguished their work from others. 'You can't just read a book,' she says. 'There are still Lakai who have giant piles of textiles. They're no longer living in yurts but their rooms are heaped with textiles up to the ceiling. It's very much a part of their lives, and we should listen to what they have to say.

'One of the things I am happiest about is that there is a new generation of scholars who have grown up outside of the Soviet educational system, like Binafsha Nodir, who helped us so much with our book on Uzbek embroidery.[9] They have the skills, the languages, the intimate knowledge of their own heritage – and the ability to ask their own grandmothers and great-grandmothers about the past. That's invaluable.'

It was a tremendous privilege, Fitz Gibbon says, to be able to travel with the freedom that they had. 'You can no longer drive a Volkswagen bus from Amsterdam to Nepal. But you can still go to a museum and learn about these cultures, to build a positive relationship from the start. And the work I do today in cultural policy is trying to ensure that access.'

1   Kate Fitz Gibbon, ed., *Who Owns the Past? Cultural Policy, Cultural Property, and the Law* (The Public Life of the Arts), Rutgers University Press, 2005.
2   Cultural Property News, www.culturalpropertynews.org
3   Kareem Abdul-Jabbar is a 7ft 2in-tall American former professional basketball player. A chapan is a man's cold-weather coat from Central Asia, often decorated with intricate threading.
4   Native to central Afghanistan, the Hazaras are an ethnic group who speak the Hazaragi dialect of Persian.
5   Samuil Martynovic Dudin (1863–1929) was an ethnographer, photographer, artist and explorer. He was a founder of the Ethnographical Department of the Russian Museum in St Petersburg and a member of several expeditions.
6   See Pip Rau, p. 42.
7   Kate Fitz Gibbon and Andrew Hale, *Ikat: The Guido Goldman Collection*, p. 16.
8   Dari denotes the Persian dialects spoken in Afghanistan.
9   Kate Fitz Gibbon and Andrew Hale, *Uzbek Embroidery in the Nomadic Tradition: The Jack and Aviva Robinson Collection*, Minneapolis Institute of Arts, 2007.

opposite
Detail of an ikat hanging, Central Asia, circa 1850–1875. The Textile Museum, 2015.11.26, Gift of Guido Goldman in honor of Bruce P. Baganz

Steven
Cohen

Photo: Rachel Meek

The accidental expert

In 1971 Steven Cohen's family expected the soft-spoken twenty-two-year-old to go into the family lumber business in Columbus, Ohio. His own impulse was to see the world. 'I sold my coin collection, which I began when I was ten years old, for a few thousand dollars,' he says. 'It was a lot of money back then, and I bought the first of several Pan Am round-the-world tickets.'

The grandson of Russian immigrants, with a newly completed college degree in Philosophy, Cohen wanted to visit ancient Buddhist archaeological sites and ponder existentialism. The lumber yard, and a promise to go to law school, were left far behind for the full year the ticket lasted. His travels would ultimately lead to his becoming an internationally renowned expert on Indian carpets. But he would encounter many dubious characters, unlikely situations and roadblocks before that happened.

Cohen's journey east began in Croatia where hustlers at the airport swiftly whisked the naïve traveller off to a bed-and-breakfast where no one spoke a word of English. 'I was starving and had no idea where I was,' he says. Instinctively, he hopped on the celebrated Orient Express to Istanbul, only to discover it wasn't the romantic train journey he'd imagined. 'It was a total disaster. There were only box cars and hard bunks full of Serbian, Croatian and Bulgarian people going back and forth to Istanbul.' He was still starving and there was no dining car; but, although it was rough, there were kind people on the train who gave him some food.

With no thought of becoming a collector or a dealer, Cohen bought his first textiles in Istanbul at the historic Grand Bazaar. The Ottoman architectural landmark houses, under its famed vaulted ceilings, hundreds of shops, restaurants, a bank, mosques, hamams and fountains. In the 1970s the bazaar became a popular destination for young travellers heading east, like Cohen, to find rides, buy dope, haggle for jewellery,

opener
Detail of an Amer carpet, north India, second half 17th century. Calouste Gulbenkian Foundation, Lisbon – Calouste Gulbenkian Museum, T61

opposite
Detail of a Katawaz embroidered bag, 20th century, Steven Cohen collection

above
Steven Cohen inspecting Mughal carpets at the Albert Hall Museum in Jaipur

carpets, textiles and ceramics, and most importantly to be part of an intriguing scene that bore no resemblance to home.

His arrival in Kabul coincided with the brutal 1971 war between East and West Pakistan. With India's support, East Pakistan won and became the independent country of Bangladesh. With no flights permitted from Kabul to India during three months of the fighting, Cohen took a room at the newly built Mustafa Hotel where he spent his days smoking 'small' amounts of marijuana and trying to teach himself to speak Dari, one of the local languages. 'I call it "baby" Dari. I basically learned nouns so I could walk into a market and buy something.'

Kabul was quiet, peaceful and calm. 'You could travel any place in the city day or night and be absolutely safe as a foreigner,' Cohen says. King Muhammad Zahir Shah was still in control (he was later overthrown in a bloodless coup by his cousin in 1973), and the place was being modernised.

Cohen wandered the Kabul markets using his limited language skills to buy things he'd never seen before, like hand-woven ikat textiles from Central Asia, silver jewellery and small, intricately embroidered bags – used for makeup, coins and other small items – made by farmers' wives in the province of Katawaz. 'I just bought the bags because I liked them and could afford them. They were cheap and colourful and no one else was seriously collecting them,' Cohen says – early evidence of his instinct for recognising unique and exceptional craft.

Flights to India resumed and Cohen completed his tour of Buddhist sites throughout most of southeast Asia. Having informed his family that neither lumber nor law were in his future, he accepted an offer to be the buyer for a couple in the Peace Corps he'd met in Kabul; since that first encounter they had established an import-export business in California.

Cohen's unassuming demeanour, trustworthy nature, and ability to buy things cheaply using his Dari, made him a perfect fit for the job in Kabul. Relishing his good fortune, he rented a big room for a year at a time on the top floor of the Mustafa Hotel, the hippie haven for London's Magic Bus passengers seeking enlightenment along the way to India and Nepal. The Mustafa, according to the first Lonely Planet guide in 1973, was 'the best place to stay... new and built around a central courtyard more like a college residence than a hotel. It's slightly expensive by Afghani standards at 60 Afs (around $1.00) for a double.'

Unlike the constant throngs of transient travellers en route to India and Nepal, Cohen stayed in Kabul for the next five years working for a string of American and Canadian dealers who appreciated the Central Asian treasures it had to offer. They wanted him to send shipments of carpets, textiles, jewellery and architectural forms like the big, carved-wood columns from Nuristan, a province in eastern Afghanistan. 'I would get up early in the morning when people from the countryside were bringing in stuff to the local dealers. They would show me what they had and

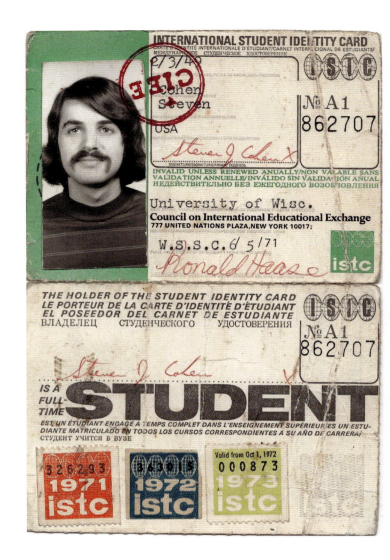

above
Steven Cohen's international student card from the early 1970s
opposite, above
Textile sellers in Afghanistan, 1970s
opposite, below
Fruit seller in Afghanistan, 1970s

sometimes I'd buy directly from them on the street.' This arrangement worked well for both of them, he explains, because 'if he didn't sell to me, the shopkeeper would give him less'. Then, Cohen would visit all the shops and have tea with the owners.

Chicken Street, with its charming row of antique shops housed in rickety two-storey wooden structures amid the live chickens, was overflowing with Central Asian carpets, textiles and all kinds of jewellery and wood objects. There he met Mustafa, a local dealer who became his main supplier.

Somewhat of a recluse, Cohen spent his evenings dining alone and reading, declining invitations from local dealers to join them at home. But over time he became a friendly fixture in town and discovered where to buy the best examples of each genre. 'If you wanted to buy a really good silk chapan [handmade men's robe worn over clothes] or a high-quality carpet, you'd go to the better antique and carpet dealers who were in other parts of Shahr-e-Naw, not just Chicken Street,' he says.

Cohen felt that it would be unethical for him to buy for himself the things he was shipping back to his employer, so he started accumulating more and more Katawaz, Hazara and Swati embroideries, since they weren't so interested in them. 'I arranged with some of the Afghan dealers to pay 100 Afghanis [Afghan currency] for a small bag which regularly sold for 30 or 40 Afghanis. In return, I would get first choice of anything I wanted regardless of the quality.' He looked for the bags every day and built one of the best collections of them in the world, which he still has.

Cohen soon discovered that his hard work and high standards were not always rewarded by those who benefited from them. For nine months he trusted to promises that he would be paid. 'It's over forty years later and I'm still waiting,' he jokes, adding that at the time it wasn't funny.

Another American dealer Cohen met was buying dhurries (flatwoven rugs, more correctly spelt daris) made in Afghan and Pakistani jails for eager buyers in New York. Cohen agreed to be his buyer. He presumed that, this time, he would be paid for his work. He quickly learned that the reason he'd been hired was because no one in Afghanistan would sell to his new boss, who owed everyone money, while they were happy to do business with Cohen since he always paid in cash.

Not suspecting that he was getting involved with another shady operator, he agreed to go to Pakistan where he would buy 'beautiful blue-and-white' dhurries in the villages around the former princely state of Bahawalpur and put them on the hippie Magic Bus to Lahore. There they would join the Afghan satrangjis he had purchased, with their bright, synthetic colours. The latter were cleaned and bleached, and then all the rugs were shipped to the US dealer.

On one of his trips, he noticed his hired taxi was being followed by a man on a bicycle. 'This was ridiculous. We were twenty miles into the

above
Detail of a Katawaz embroidered puttee, one of a pair, 20th century, Steven Cohen collection

opposite
Katawaz embroidered bag, 20th century, Steven Cohen collection

desert and he's on a bicycle. We'd come back hours later and we'd see him still trying to follow us.' Back at the American Embassy in Kabul, Cohen was told they were looking for a suspected drug dealer. This was not surprising since, according to Cohen, the majority of American carpet and textile dealers in Afghanistan then were also drug dealers, 'stuffing hash into posteen' – the pungent sheepskin coat worn by Afghan Pushtun tribes – to disguise the smell. The coats would then be sent to the US where they were very popular with young people in the counter-culture. The US Embassy in Kabul had asked the Pakistani police to follow the suspect, who was older and named Steven L. Cohen. Despite the mistaken identity, the police continued to follow Steven J. Cohen, bringing an abrupt end to his Pakistani forays, since no one would sell to a suspected drug dealer being followed by the police.

Cohen's familiar face in Kabul and good negotiating skills could have worked against him, because he was to be paid on commission. 'The longer I was there, the cheaper I could buy things, so I would have got next to nothing. But since I never received a penny from this dealer, either, it didn't matter,' he says.

On his third try, Cohen managed to work for a more reliable Canadian buyer, even briefly going to work in her store in Victoria, on the west coast of British Columbia. 'I could sell anything,' he says, 'because I really liked the stuff. I believed in its value.' He returned to Kabul and continued buying for her until 1976 when he was ready for a change. By then Kabul was crawling with tourists, as more of the Baby Boomer generation were graduating from university and joining the hippie trail to points east.

Cohen's experience with unscrupulous American dealers had not worked out financially. But his willingness to take a risk with them in Afghanistan provided exceptional opportunities to learn about regional carpets and textiles, experience that otherwise he may not have had. His work also provided monetary benefits to local dealers who, he learned, had been buying and selling things their whole lives and welcomed a foreigner's interest. 'There were always carpet dealers in Afghanistan. They didn't just suddenly become dealers when the latest round of Westerners appeared.

'I probably shipped out 300 Turkmen and Baluch carpets, bag faces and tent bands. That's what was available in the 1970s, although most of the really great pieces had been out of Turkmenistan for 100 years,' he says, noting that the Russians had previously brought out a huge amount. 'I was a foreigner and was thus asked to pay more, but

above
Detail of a Katawaz embroidered puttee, 20th century, Steven Cohen collection
opposite
Detail of a Katawaz embroidery, 20th century, Steven Cohen collection

above
Chicken Street in Kabul, Afghanistan, 1970s

I expected that and was willing to do so since I could afford it and suspected I would end up with something exceptionally good.

'In 1973 I was buying silver at a cheap price because there had been a three-year drought. People were forced to sell their silver or they would have starved,' he says, adding that they had always considered silver jewellery something to keep for an emergency and sell when necessary. 'Their grandparents would have understood it perfectly well – it wasn't unusual to them in their culture, although a Westerner may be confused by the willingness to sell off family heirlooms.'

All three of the Western-based dealers he worked for went on to establish successful stores in North America that lasted for decades, helping to generate a new interest in the rare and beautiful materials Cohen found and sent them. 'It initiated an interest that wouldn't otherwise be there,' he says. 'Those objects had always been in Afghanistan but they hadn't always been traded, classified, sold for money and put in people's collections. They're beautiful objects and they became valuable.' Some of his Afghan dealers, with whom he remains friends, eventually moved to Pakistan, the US and Australia to escape the decades of violent conflict caused by foreign occupation, civil war, religious extremism and terrorism, which destroyed their businesses and threatened their lives.

Back in the US, Cohen's penchant for accepting dodgy promises led him, once again, to more remarkable situations. He moved to Ojai, California after hearing from friends that the famous ninety-year-old Beatrice Wood – a theosophist, potter, former actress and ballerina in Paris, known as the 'Mama of Dada' for her association with the French artist Marcel Duchamp – needed a curator for her 'Museum & Library of World Folk Art'. Once there, he discovered that the so-called institute didn't actually exist, and instead of a curator she really needed somebody to look after her.

'I'm doing all the cooking, cleaning and vacuuming and not getting paid anything except free room and board,' he says, describing a familiar pattern. He was also selling the ceramics she produced from a little showroom she had in her home. 'The bodies of the ceramics were terrible but the glazes were incredible,' he says, 'and people were coming and buying them.' Cohen suspected that Wood's powerful dealers were storing up her work and were waiting to profit from it when she died. That would mean that he was selling off their future earnings and giving the money to her. It would also explain why he was abruptly fired from the job after an apparent intervention.

Unsure what to do next, he heard that the owners of a pink mansion, in the historic Presidio district of San Francisco, needed a house sitter because the family lived elsewhere. No sooner had he moved in than the entire family moved back. Suddenly he was cooking and cleaning for them, and chauffeuring the elderly matriarch back and forth to the opera in her gold Rolls-Royce. She was a wealthy heiress and a descendant of a family given

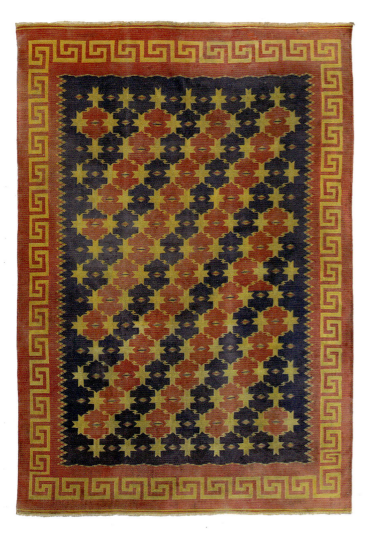

above
Dhurrie, India, first half 20th century,
Yogesh Chaudhary collection
opposite
Detail of one of the first ikat textiles,
consisting of three joined narrow
panels, that Steven Cohen bought in
Kabul in the early 1970s

land grants back when Spain still owned Mexico and what is now the southwestern United States. 'I became a really good cook,' he says, although his pattern of financial exploitation continued. 'I worked for forty-two days at minimum wage without a day off.'

After the death, in 1976, of his grandfather, whose fortune and heart attacks coincided with the rise and fall of the stock market, he decided to stop being exploited and use his inheritance to go to graduate school. He wanted to study the little-known antique ikat textiles from Uzbekistan that he loved and had been buying for years in Kabul. 'I didn't find any academics who knew what they were, where or how they were made, or anything about their history,' he says. Unable to locate a single American university that considered carpets or Asian textiles an academic subject, he applied to the School of Oriental and African Studies (SOAS) at the University of London, England.

Despite his first-hand experience with the esoteric ikat textiles, he was viewed unfavourably by the head of the Central Asian and Persian Department because he knew only Dari – a variety of the Persian Farsi language spoken in Afghanistan – rather than proper Farsi. According to her this wasn't up to standard, even though language wasn't a requirement for admission. He was stumped as to what he should do. However, an American friend he had met in Kabul suggested he apply to the SOAS South Asia Department since, according to him, 'they'll take anyone'. Although he knew nothing about Indian carpets or textiles, he was, indeed, accepted.

At the time it didn't seem like it, but the rejection of Cohen's initial application was a stroke of good fortune. Russia's invasion of Afghanistan in 1979 meant he would not have been able to undertake any field research there or in the rest of Central Asia, including Uzbekistan, because those places became off limits to Westerners. 'It's all luck,' he says, musing that his life would have been very different if he hadn't kept in touch with the friend whose casual suggestion sent him down an entirely new path.

Cohen arrived at SOAS in the autumn of 1977 in a department that included Sri Lanka, India, Pakistan and Nepal, but not Afghanistan. 'Now I'm in the Indian section – I'm registered for the art and archaeology of South Asia – and I didn't know anything about Mughal or Indian carpets,' he says. 'My proposal was to study dhurries, which my advisor, a former British Army Ghurkha in India, referred to as "Indian bath mats".'

After three years studying Indian art and archaeology as well as related Persian subjects, and visiting around thirty jails in India to see the dhurries made there, Cohen concluded that they weren't an academic subject, after all. He switched to a much more esoteric dissertation topic – the appearance of carpets in Indian miniature paintings before Akbar, the third Mughal Emperor, who reigned from 1556–1603.

His new topic betrayed a certain sense of mischief. 'It's a trick thing, because there are no surviving Indian carpets before Akbar.' The only

Photo: Jim McHugh

above
Beatrice Wood in her Ojai studio, 1983
opposite
Katawaz embroidered bags, 20th century, Steven Cohen collection

available references for study before 1603 are the literature and representations of carpets in miniature paintings. 'I would have no competition, since no one else in the world was working on such a silly subject,' he says.

The study of carpets, in general, was not a recognised academic field and there was very little work, specifically, on Mughal carpets. Cohen's pioneering research helped legitimise the academic study of carpets. 'As far as I know Dan Walker, at Harvard, and I were the only two people studying Mughal carpets, although he was working with real carpets and I was working with their history.' He credits his advisor, John Burton-Page, the reader in Indian languages and art and archaeology of South Asia at SOAS, and to a lesser extent Robert Skelton, the then head of the Indian section at London's Victoria and Albert Museum, for their support of his initiative.

In the midst of his PhD studies, Cohen took a break in 1980 to work as assistant editor at HALI, then a fledgling magazine but which would become the pre-eminent publication on antique carpets. He left HALI when SOAS required him to complete his dissertation, which needed his full attention. 'I did actually turn it in,' he confirms, dusting off a copy of 'The Development of Indian Floor Coverings and Their Appearance in Miniature Paintings'. In 1986 he became Dr Cohen, and an independent textile historian. 'I make house calls,' he jokes, although he is more likely to be found deep in the storage rooms of museums analysing their textiles and carpets.

He is especially interested in the technical aspects, he says, because physical properties are facts. 'If I look at the warp and see multi-stranded cotton, then I know it's an Indian carpet. If it only has three or four strands in a cotton warp then I know it's not north Indian.' Cohen praises the late Dr Jon Thompson, author and former May Beattie Fellow in Carpet Studies at the University of Oxford, as a pioneer in structural analysis and with cementing its status as an academic subject.

Cohen's emphasis on the importance of structure goes back to his days in Afghanistan. 'I worked for people who made up stories when they didn't know where a carpet was from or the date it was made. That irritates me – so many dealers know so little about their subjects.' He insists on fact-based evidence to support his analysis. 'What I've learned over forty years is that you don't say anything about a textile until you've actually analysed it and seen what it's made of. Then you start speculating on the basis of comparative analysis. You find a certain dye, for example, and it eliminates all the other things that it can't possibly be. It narrows it down to what it is.'

If that sounds boring, Cohen doesn't care. His hard line on fact-based analysis has given him a reputation for honesty and made him a reliable authority in a field where there are often many opinions and little to support them. 'People know I'm interested academically and historically and I'll give them an honest answer.' He believes there has been some opening up in academia towards the study of textiles, but not so much towards carpets. Museums are changing somewhat, too, he says, with curators becoming more interested in carpets and textiles, and in their technical aspects. Overall, however, he says that carpets are still neglected, partly 'because they're big, heavy and they attract moths'.

A highly sought-after expert, Cohen continues to conduct independent research, consult with private collectors and museums, write exhibition catalogues, and give lectures and papers at various symposia around the world. He frequently visits India where he has collaborated on several catalogues for the well-known TAPI Collection in Surat.

What still comes through strongly, after over forty years, is Cohen's enduring excitement and curiosity at seeing a beautiful textile. 'Once I like one, I want to know more about it,' he says, pointing at the first ikat he ever bought years ago in Kabul. 'I've never seen another one like it.'

He and his partner, Rosemary Crill – a prolific author and former senior curator for South Asia at the Victoria and Albert Museum – both love ikat, he says, and they collect it all over the world. 'We buy things we can afford and we don't mind if it's a fragment of something.' With a full line-up of textile-related activity on the calendar, Cohen, now seventy-four, jokes that he would prefer working in the garden and cooking – two more of the many interests and skills he picked up on the long and winding road he followed to Indian carpets.

opposite
Detail of an embroidered Hazara bag, 20th century, Steven Cohen collection

Connecting the world:
Designers and influencers

From the 1970s to the 2000s, small, speciality boutiques, sometimes owned by the dealers themselves, sprang up in big cities like London, New York and Los Angeles. These shops catered to a select clientele, many of whom had travelled to the same places as the dealers, customers who were happy to buy a familiar reminder of their trip. Most people, however, had never seen, and were unaccustomed to, the unique motifs, unusual colourways and varieties of textiles, robes, shawls and carpets that poured in from Asia during those years.

The role of inspired and inventive interior and textile designers and other influencers was crucial in determining whether and where they were used. Most notable is Robert Kime, the British interior decorator who for decades has fine-tuned his particular style, in which antique and vintage carpets and textiles feature widely. Known for saying that he will invariably start a room with a rug, Kime has attracted clients as varied as Prince Charles, Andrew Lloyd Webber and Tory Burch. The 'Kime look' soon became so popular that it morphed into its own category of style. Its originator is routinely cited as a source, if not the source, of inspiration for a new generation of designers. This chapter features some of the American, British and European designers and influencers in this vein who, enamoured by dazzling antique and vintage materials, have found fresh and contemporary ways to introduce them into homes across the world.

The dealers exporting these goods from the East to the West were able to gain some understanding of the cultures that produced them from living with the people who made, used, collected and sold them. Their knowledge grew through their daily encounters in the markets and bazaars with the local shopkeepers, traders, pickers and families they got to know over the years.

Western-based designers, primarily with an art-history or design-school background, often had no knowledge of these cultures or their histories. They were first drawn to the textiles and carpets for their aesthetic and visual appeal – the daring colour palettes, the bold motifs, the sensuous velvets, silks and linen fabrics – and their educated eyes recognised the unique artistic qualities and artisanship of the intricate embroidery, elaborate dyeing techniques and expertly executed weaving.

After discovering the beauty of these materials, these designers actively pursued their interest in them, often establishing personal collections in addition to incorporating their finds professionally. They hunted for them wherever they could – rummaging through boutiques, flea markets and trade shows, and travelling themselves, to be educated, inspired and to enhance their collections.

London's **Robert Kime** says that his early clients knew nothing about what they were seeing other than that they liked it. Often dealing out of his home and buildings on his property, Kime opened a shop in Oundle with Miriam Rothschild in 1966. He opened his first shop in London in 2001 and a second one in 2016

opener
Detail of a chair upholstered in *Termez Blue*, a hand-dyed ikat fabric designed by Robert Kime

opposite
Abbey sofa by Robert Kime, upholstered in an antique weave and pictured in an interior featuring the wealth of textiles for which Robert Kime is known

where antique carpets, cushions and furniture, upholstered with kilims, suzanis, ikat and other antique textiles, provided a first look, for many, at these imported materials and an impression of how they could be used in their own homes.

American interior designer **Frank de Biasi** was head of interiors from 1992–2004 at the New York firm Peter Marino Architect. 'Our clients were Europeans, Americans and interested collectors, and we were influencing them,' he says. 'They loved to see something different, fun, adventurous.'

However, carpet and textile designer **Madeline Weinrib** reports that her early cotton flatweave rugs were not an immediate success. The *Zig Zag* was one of her first creations, and it took six months to sell the first one. 'My designs were seen as very aggressive,' she says. 'Things that are new and different do not immediately excite people. It was really when we showed people how to use them that they took off.'

Italian interior designer **Nicolò Castellini Baldissera** also found that certain clients needed some persuasion. 'The old pieces speak to a very small circle of clients – to aficionados,' he says. 'Often the beaten, lived-in look doesn't appeal.'

Graham Head, former president and vice chair of New York's ABC Carpet & Home furnishing emporium, says that he noticed a backlash against computerised perfection. 'Young New York consumers living in Tribeca and SoHo wanted something unique. They didn't need wall-to-wall any more [owing to the advent of central heating and air conditioning], so it wasn't difficult to sell beautiful rugs.' The ABC motto – 'Collect, Don't Decorate' – soon reflected the new mood.

Keith Recker was working, in the 1990s, in home furnishings and fashion accessories at big commercial retail outlets like Gump's in San Francisco, Saks Fifth Avenue and Bloomingdale's in New York. His corporate experience was very different from Head's at the family-owned ABC. 'Quite honestly there was a deep unawareness around the office, even when we were dealing with carpets. I noticed that my colleagues had no textile vocabulary, but I was always passionate about them, it was important to me. Who knows what I might have coaxed into the marketplace from my passion?'

Robert Kime

The clients of Robert Kime range from personal friends and neighbours to members of the British aristocracy and numerous celebrities. He has been an antique dealer and decorator for over fifty years. After stints at Sotheby's and working for the Rothschild family, he sold antiques out of his home for a number of years and started decorating interiors when visitors to his home said they'd like their house to look like his.

As a student at Oxford, Kime studied medieval history after travelling for eighteen months to France and Italy to learn languages, and to Greece and Masada, Israel, to take part in archaeological digs. His deep sense of history is what informs his decorating. 'Oxford taught me I was not a scholar – I really could not sit in the library for eight hours … but I have never tired of looking at objects that inform me of the past.'

He acquired his first Iranian carpet when he was twelve years old. 'I went in and paid £5 and I bought it.' He grew up in a home where his mother and grandmother had surrounded their lives with colour and quality furniture. His mother, he claims, was 'a worse collector than I am'. While he was an undergraduate,

his mother suddenly needed to raise money quickly. Kime achieved that for her by selling furniture, largely inherited from his grandmother, out of his student rooms at Oxford. The experience was the start of his lifelong career dealing in antiques.

Kime is a zealot for fabrics that 'resonate with the past', and travel was the best way to discover them. 'You find things you'd never see otherwise,' he says describing the excitement of stumbling upon antique textiles 'with their irresistible quality' just lying around the markets in places like Istanbul and Bukhara. For him, such venerable fabrics seem ageless. Closer to home, Kime would wake up at 3 a.m. and drive all night in order to arrive at Manchester in time for the 6 a.m. opening of the fabric markets held there. 'You could see wonderful things,' he says.

When Kime starts to work with a client, they look at the fabrics he has designed. Once the client has picked out six of them, he says, he can tell who they are, what they are and where they come from. 'It tells me all I need to know about what they want,' he says. He has no rules about mixing and matching – simple fabrics

opposite
Hand-dyed ikat fabric designed by Robert Kime
left
Enford daybed by Robert Kime, upholstered in an antique Turkish weave

mix magically with others that he collected over many years of travel and exploration. Anatolian tent hangings become curtains, West African kente cloths cover ottomans, Italian mezzaro hangings drape beds and lampshades are swathed in antique silks. Upon seeing one of his creations, former First Lady Nancy Reagan remarked 'It's marvellous, nothing matches!'

Textiles, he says, provide physical relief and calm a room down, 'even if you wouldn't think it was anything to do with the textiles. They resonate with history, and if you can connect it to the past it gives you a feeling of strength. If everything was modern you wouldn't have any sense of the past at all. Textiles give you a feeling of the communities they come from.'

Nicolò Castellini Baldissera

'My love is much greater than my knowledge,' says Nicolò Castellini Baldissera. 'I'm not a scholar or a textile expert but I use them a lot. My first attraction is the colour – that plays the main role for me. Colours that you would never dream of matching come together so beautifully and perfectly balanced. With these fabrics and textiles, you have more freedom of mismatching colours. I forgive it completely in them.'

Castellini Baldissera is attracted to old fabrics and consciously seeks them out at auction and wherever he travels. This ensures a ready supply while building up knowledge of where to find what he wants when needed. 'New pieces don't have a tenth of the charm that those old pieces have,' he insists.

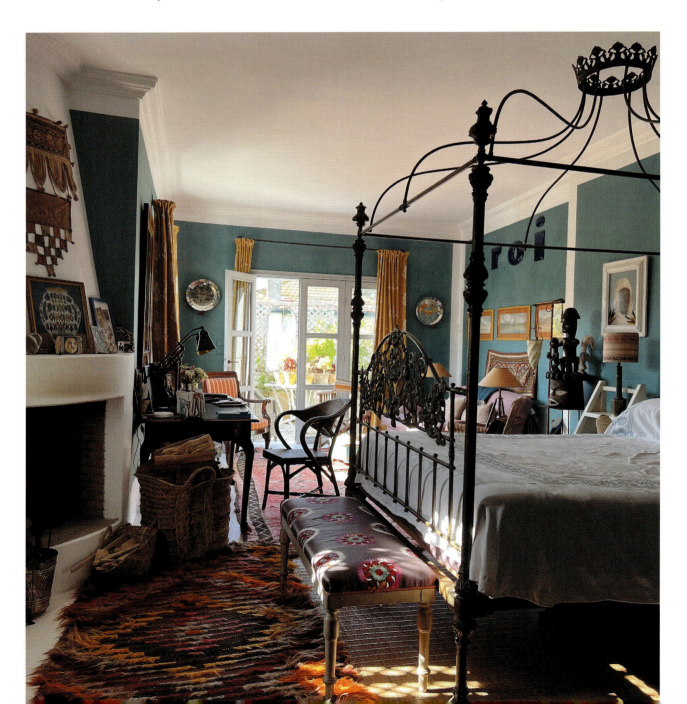

Many of these designers grew up in a family with a long textile or carpet history. Castellini Baldissera was born in Milan in his ancestral home, Casa degli Atellani, restored by his great grandfather, renowned architect Piero Portaluppi, and residence of his father, prominent architect and co-founder of C&C Milano Fabric Company. The company has continued to branch out for 150 years. It offers elegant silk, linen and other fabrics for home interiors from stores in Milan, Paris and New York. In addition to his interior design work, Castellini Baldiserra designs new rugs produced in India and Nepal for Fedora, a New York-based company, where he provides 'design inspiration' and collaborates on colour selection.

His first trip to India was with his father in the 1990s. Since then he has travelled many times to Turkey, where he bought his first rug. In 2010 he moved to Tangier, Morocco, where he mixes local style with disparate global influences. His books *Inside Tangier* and *Inside Milan* showcase homes that, like him, embrace a love of antique textiles blending colour, pattern and taste.

For his more traditional clients, he mixes the old with modern fabrics and rugs, often in places least expected, like Turkish kilims in a Swiss chalet. He also will combine carpets from very different places – Moroccan from the Rif mountains and filikli from Turkey – giving an unusual patchwork effect.

Madeline Weinrib

Weinrib was an artist before she started designing her own line of dhurrie carpets and ikat textiles. 'I approached it as an artist, not a rug maker. I was using motifs like mandalas that were traditional and ancient. I was interested in how many ways I could play with colour with the mandala. It was exciting and fun. I never thought anybody was ever going to see my rugs.'

Weinrib comes from a fourth generation of carpet sellers going back to 1897 when her great grandfather, an immigrant from Austria, began peddling used linoleum and carpets from a pushcart on New York's Lower East Side. Her grandfather subsequently opened up ABC Carpet and her father, who started selling carpets in 1947, moved the store to Union Square in 1961. The store expanded to include another space across the street which Weinrib's sister, Paulette Cole, turned into a chic home-furnishing emporium in the 1980s, filling it with antiques and accessories found on her travels.

Despite her family history, Weinrib had no intention of getting into the rug or textile business. 'I was spending a lot of time in Asia, exploring and meeting different artisans. I was just dabbling in textiles. At first I was not thinking about making rugs, then I became obsessed with making rugs, and then I thought I would never stop making them.' She set up her own studio in ABC Carpet & Home on the top floor where the carpets were sold. 'Working in the back of that floor was really magical because of all the beautiful imported rugs and the opportunity to look at them,' she says.

Weinrib was originally viewing flatwoven rugs in India from a Western perspective. 'I was exploring ways

that would make them feel unique rather than trying to reproduce the original. Great design should have flexibility,' she says. Then her future husband, Graham Head, showed her a swatch of ikat he had brought back from one of his trips; he mentioned that the unique weaving technique was being resurrected in Uzbekistan. She became curious and decided to pursue it. Google her name today, and her ikat and suzani fabrics and pillows are sure to come up. Whether working with traditional artisans from India for dhurries or from Uzbekistan for suzani and ikat textiles, her approach was the same. Using traditional motifs, she simplified and pared them to their essence, making them appear both very modern and quite traditional at once.

'I made what they made, but I came from a totally different point of view,' she says. 'I looked at what was traditional, I looked at the language. My designs were very much based on the traditional motifs, just a slightly different scale. But my colour choices were contemporary. I was thinking about how this could be used in a Western home.' Eventually, she says, her decision to put a modern spin on something very traditional brought in a whole new audience. 'I was making global designs exactly when the world was becoming more connected.'

Graham Head

Graham Head declares: 'I felt passionately about every piece I bought for ABC. I always bought every rug as though it was for myself. I would also buy two or three textiles on every buying trip I made for my own collection.' He became one of the biggest buyers

of antique carpets, spending more than thirty years with ABC.

His career began when he needed a job after travelling, and saw there was a vacancy in the rug department at the store in London where he was training. From there he moved in the late 1980s to Oriental Carpet Manufacturers – for a long time the world's largest buyer and producer of carpets, established by British merchants in 1907 in Smyrna (known today as Izmir). With his move to New York and ABC, Head was in the right place at the right time for a carpet and textile buyer. The 1979 Iranian revolution and the Russian invasion of Afghanistan saw a sudden inrush of goods. People were forced to sell family heirlooms as they fled conflict in those countries. The fall of the Iron Curtain in 1989 opened the floodgates after fifty years of Russian rule in Central Asia.

New York is a furnishing centre that attracts designers and decorators, and ABC provided a unique resource. 'One of the appeals was that we sold everything from dhurries for $100 to antique Persian carpets for $100,000,' says Head. 'I'd buy all sorts of stuff on trips from China to North Africa. There were no rules. I could buy whatever I liked.' This, he says, was because ABC's owner, the late Jerome Weinrib, was equally passionate. 'He loved the carpets and textiles and had confidence in the market for them.'

At ABC, customers could see a mix of vintage-textile-covered cushions, random antique textile fragments and antique carpets scattered throughout the six floors of the store, casually thrown over the backs of contemporary sofas and chairs, coffee tables and counter tops, and billowy vintage saris hanging as curtains. 'It was part theatre, part retail,' says Head about ABC's unique in-store curation, often referred to as a living magazine filled with inspiration and discovery. 'We combined vintage and contemporary. We mixed and matched to show people how to do it.'

Keith Recker

Keith Recker has his aunt to thank for introducing him to textile traditions at a young age. 'She was one of those hippies who made that trek,' he says, recalling her travels overland from India to Iran in the 1970s. Something of the counter-culture ethos may have rubbed off on him, too. In 1999 he took a break from his commercial jobs to

be director of Aid to Artisans, travelling to Central Asia to evaluate a US government-funded support programme for artists and craftspeople. By 2005 he was done with retail. Since then he has co-founded *Hand/Eye* magazine and been creative director of the International Folk Art Market in Santa Fe. He is editor in chief of *TABLE Magazine* and also the author of two books on colour: *The Shades that Shape Our Souls* and *True Colors: World Masters of Natural Dyes and Pigments*.

Frank de Biasi

Frank de Biasi credits his former boss, architect and avid textile collector Peter Marino, with opening his eyes to what was going on around the world. 'We would collect and buy things all over,' de Biasi says, acknowledging the late Cora Ginsburg, one of New York's most prominent textile collectors and dealers, as a particular inspiration among the many enthusiasts who had sprung into action. 'Whatever caught our eye and inspired us would be interesting – colour, texture, weave, condition. Different people had different specialities,' he notes, mentioning Pip Rau and Joss Graham in London. It was in the flea markets of Paris that he bought the most textiles, often French ones with designs originating in India.

De Biasi creates textiles with completely different functions from their original purpose, and may also alter the size and colour of the printed pattern to better suit a design need. Taking inspiration from a vintage document but altering it, he says, is 'a way of incorporating antique and vintage in a modern way to create something new.'

Authenticity and sustainability

For collectors, authenticity and provenance are the most important factors. Such people make every effort to conserve a piece in its original condition, even if it's just a fragment, in a nod to cultural history and to maintain market value. A designer's criteria are quite different. Visual appeal is the primary focus for pieces that will be mixed and matched in modern settings. They use antique and vintage textiles and carpets whole or cut, folded, stitched or reproduced, to fit customised upholstered pieces for specific spaces, often in a mix-and-match of old and new.

opposite
Interior featuring fabrics and furnishings by Madeline Weinrib

Nicolò Castellini Baldissera is a master at combining antique and contemporary pieces. He likes to transform old textiles into decorating accessories – cushions, bedspreads, upholstery, curtains – maintaining their integrity when he can. 'I'm very respectful of the work behind each piece. I try to use the fabric in a certain way. I don't cut it, I fold it,' he says. 'I used a suzani in my bathroom – it was a square and I needed something rectangular, so I folded it in half and stitched it. I wouldn't have the heart to ruin such beautiful work.'

Asian designs have also been the inspiration for adaptations that appeal to European and North American tastes. Furthermore they offer sustainability, as supplies of original pieces become scarce. While decorating some of England's foremost houses, Kime has seen his large stock of antique textiles begin to dwindle. 'I was only finding enough material for cushions, not curtains,' he says.

This led him in 1983 to begin designing his own fabrics, which now number approximately 350, based on his extensive collection. 'Document pieces' of antique and vintage textiles – some as small as the size of a handkerchief – are central to his designs, which he calls interpretations. 'I'm trying to get the essence of what they are, the history behind a pattern and fabric. Sometimes I'll enlarge the pattern, sometimes I'll reduce it. I'll fiddle around with it until it fits what I need at the time.' Most of Kime's interpretations are hand-printed or woven in England, while his ikats and embroideries are executed in Uzbekistan.

The influence of these decorating and design visionaries goes far beyond their own clients and reverberates from couture fashion houses to discount department stores, where mass-produced, block-printed textiles can be found stacked on the shelves and where machine-made carpets incorporating Asian designs abound.

While many welcomed these fresh designs and imported textiles, not everyone has been so admiring. The use of certain designs has occasionally brought accusations of cultural appropriation, defined as an unacknowledged use of another's culture and heritage while leaving them out of the story.

Over the past two decades fashion brands accused of appropriation have faced public criticism and lawsuits. Yet cross-cultural design inspiration goes back centuries. The early days of global trade opened the door to cultural exchange – expanding commerce, bringing textiles to new markets and allowing never-before-seen novelties to inspire designs. According to American cultural commentator Virginia Postrel:

With the flourishing trade of the Mongol Empire, designs migrated across cultural boundaries, combining a mixture of traditional Chinese motifs, Middle Eastern elements and local Central Asian repertoires. Entire colonies of skilled artisans of mixed ethnicity were created, which facilitated a kind of hybrid development in textile art and its technology – bewildering textile historians today.'[1]

Keith Recker has worked with the annual International Folk Art Market in Santa Fe, which supports artisans around the world; he says it's complicated. 'I don't think the notion of authenticity was a driving force much before the Victorian era, if at all. We have been creating new standards in the past few years, and it's probably overdue that we do that – but using that filter on things prior to the imposition of these new standards is problematic.'

Questions of appropriation and authenticity continue to roil, and brands incorporating imagery and designs from other cultures must now be more conscious of their origins. Not everyone agrees, however, on who or what defines 'authenticity'. Postrel argues that consumers, not producers, determine the meaning and value of textiles. 'The cultural authenticity of cloth arises not from the purity of its origins but from the ways in which individuals and groups turn textiles to their own purpose. Trying to impose an external standard, heedless of consumers' beliefs and desires, is not merely futile but disrespectful and absurd.'[2]

Increased demand for indigenous designs and materials has also had an impact on the supply side, according to Recker. 'There was a certain amount of cultural exploration that happened through the 1970s, 1980s and 1990s with the introduction of authentic vintage or antique materials that were being brought back. Their influence was restricted to individuals who

opposite
Silbury sofa by Robert Kime, photographed on an antique carpet and surrounded by furnishings in Kime fabrics, new and repurposed

appreciated the craft. But by the 2000s you're not buying something imported from India, you're buying a reproduction that's more about commerce. It was cut-and-paste.'

Technological innovation in order to make textiles more widely available began long ago. When France banned the importation of hand-printed cotton fabrics known as calico from India, new technologies were devised to produce replacements. By the mid-17th century printing techniques had been developed throughout Europe that, if not quite matching the quality of the Indian originals, satisfied the home market.

The antique and vintage pieces long sought by collectors and designers alike come from an era when some of these materials were integral aspects of cultural practices and the ability to make them widespread. A range of factors over the past century – mechanisation, globalisation, urban migration, mass marketing, increased travel, climate change – led to major cultural and population shifts and the near disappearance of textile skills in some places. 'There's a strong argument to be made that people at both senior and junior levels have lost a lot of textile knowledge,' says Recker. But there is another side to the coin. While there is no single explanation for it, the heightened interest in ikat, suzanis, block prints, kilims, tribal carpets and other traditional designs and materials has generated a revival of these artisanal crafts throughout Asia.

The lifestyles of the peoples who originated these valued artefacts have changed, perhaps for ever. But local groups, often supported by governments, international non-government organisations or private international donors, are revitalising the traditional skills of embroidery, weaving and natural dyeing.

1   Virginia Postrel. *The Fabric of Civilization: How Textiles Made the World*, Basic Books, New York, 2020, p. 185.
2   Ibid, p. 203.

Since my interview, Robert Kime has sadly passed on. Robert Kime Ltd. continues to operate following Robert's design ethos, and his legacy lives on in fabrics, wallpapers, furniture and lighting by Robert Kime as well as the many spaces he decorated and the generations of interior designers he inspired

opposite
Dyed threads drying as part of the textile-making process in Uzbekistan, where old craft traditions are now being revitalised

Ambassadors and adventurers

The archivist, curator and historian Mary Schoeser MA FRSA has had access to numerous public and private collections across the UK, Europe and America. Among her official positions she is honorary president of the Textile Society (UK) and affiliated with the Victoria and Albert Museum as an honorary senior research fellow. Her many publications include the books Textiles: The Art of Mankind *and* World Textiles: A Concise History. *Here she places the textile collectors we meet in these pages in the context of their historical predecessors, assessing their contribution to the modern world's understanding of diverse textile cultures.*

I once said when talking about textile collections that 'If you stand and listen very carefully ... you hear the voices from the past, the stories of sweat and tears, pride and years of work to perfect a skill. You just have to pay attention...'[1] Between the lines of the stories within this book, much attests to that kind of listening. The objects prized for their beauty or ability to inspire new products have reached us as a result of both courage and selflessness. There's the risk-taking of the travelling but, as well, the determined honouring of the makers themselves.

That honouring takes several forms. One is the considerable contribution to our knowledge of non-Western textiles through publications. The most prolific writer interviewed here has been John Gillow, whose WorldCat entry produces fifty-two results.[2] In a world where traditional ways of life, and the textiles and skills associated with them, are disappearing fast, the importance of recording these things for posterity cannot be overstated. Another way in which the creators of textile treasures are honoured is through aiding the revival of traditional forms. It was more than twenty years ago that Elizabeth Hewitt began her work to seek out and support traditional ikat makers. Today there are many others like her who continue to ensure that true respect for makers is at the heart of what they do.

There is a long tradition of ambassadors, both official and unofficial, who have contributed to the voyages taken by textile cultures.[3] One need only look at the late 17th-century French publication *Le Mercure galant*,[4] the first to include fashion plates. These illustrations make clear that *siamoise*, the term for cloths made in imitation of Thailand's distinctive striped, multi-fibre cloths, was introduced to the court of Louis XIV in 1686 by ambassador Kosa Pa's delegation at the behest of King Narai.

Such linguistic tributes can also be found in garments such as banyan, precursor of the dressing gown, whose name can be traced from the Gujarati for trader, back to the Portuguese *banean*, probably from Tamil *vaniyan*, from Sanskrit *vānija* from an Iranian tree of the species under which traders did business. Printed cottons have been known in France for centuries as *indiennes*. Both of the latter are, of course, the result of trade, driven not solely by political interests, but dependent on the merchant adventurers who braved difficult seas and

opener
Petticoat panel, made in India for the Dutch market, where the textile would most likely have been incorporated into everyday wear for a wealthy farmer's wife during the third quarter of the 18th century. Metropolitan Museum of Art, 1992.82, Purchase, Friends of European Sculpture and Decorative Arts Gifts, 1992

opposite
Banyan (at-home robe), India for the Western market, circa 1750. LACMA, M.2005.42, Costume Council Fund

arduous land passages to bring textile treasures to Western consumers.

The 17th-century merchant adventurers not only transformed the market but also encouraged the development of local imitations. Their manner of dressing changed male attire for ever. Imagine the stereotypical pirate; he wears what in England and France was called a Persian vest (in reality an Ottoman outer garment), and it slowly evolved into the Western man's suit.

A more recent example of textile ambassadorship is the Afghan coat made famous by the Beatles in late 1966. In October 1966 Craig Sams began importing them into London, selling to several boutiques. It was Granny Takes a Trip, on the King's Road, that alerted Sams to the need for more, since the Beatles had left the shop wearing them. It seemed that every rock star donned one in 1967. Sams recalls:

> Within a few weeks no sheep between Istanbul and Kabul was safe – suddenly they were worth more for their skins than for their meat as people hastily killed them, skinned them, did machine stitched embroidery or quick hand stitching and rushed them to the UK and other countries where the market was booming.[5]

What began in 1960s North America as medieval fairs – often intermingled with music festivals, appearing like a sea of tie-dyed T-shirts and Indian block-printed cotton throws – gradually became textile and tribal arts shows. For a few days hundreds of exhibitors gathered, treating thousands of visitors to the sight and touch of remarkable objects. Critically, the result was a wider and more sophisticated understanding and appreciation of substance and structure, from the type and number of knots per inch to the distinction between stitches or dyeing methods.

Among these shows were two launched in the mid-1980s Californian Bay Area. The former hippie hangout of Marin County saw the birth of the American Indian Art Show in 1984. It is now held in San Francisco, where the Tribal and Textile Art Show first opened its doors in 1986. It should come as no surprise that both shows, together with the similarly named events in Santa Fe,

are the work of a partnership that includes John Morris, famous for his involvement in the production of the original Woodstock Festival in 1969 and ownership of the Rainbow Theatre, London's foremost rock music venue for a decade from 1971.[6] Here is more evidence of the importance of those who act as ambassadors, in this case providing 'non-curated', less formal, more immediate access to tribal textiles.

Dr Steven Cohen, having initially supplied several North American gallerists, became an authority on the history of Mughal carpets and is just one of those who became conduits between the real objects, their techniques and narratives on the one hand, and museums, private collectors and 'amateur' devotees. His stint as an assistant editor of HALI, not long after it was founded in London in 1978, also prompts recognition of this magazine's critical impact as an emissary for that nascent movement towards a genuine regard for carpets and world textiles, which continues today.

Many of the people featured in these pages, like Pip Rau, Andy Hale, Kate Fitz Gibbon and Joss Graham, have helped to expand major museum collections, allowing such institutions to incorporate textile types that had previously been dismissed as folk art not properly belonging in their collections. Their names often pop up in provenance records in online databases; either they sold or donated pieces directly to a museum, or a private collector bought from them before subsequently gifting the piece. The tangible fruits of these 20th-century adventurers' travels are therefore now shared with a larger public, inspiring appreciation of other cultures.

———

It is no accident that textiles have been travelling the known worlds for millennia. This volume provides invaluable insights into the means by which this has happened since the 1960s, but archaeological evidence of their trade remains from as early as 8,000 to 9,000 years ago. This should surprise no one, for textiles are created to *move*. Aside from being able to swathe the body, they are the first portable and colourful materials. Long before the arrival of film and television, textiles furnished fluid imagery, providing the banners and flags that accompanied pageants and armies alike. The stuff

of identity and memory, they were equally articulate whether used for nomadic yurts or in religious sanctuaries.

We begin to have ample visual documentation of textile travels with the blossoming of a particular genre of portable textiles: medieval tapestries. Among the best-known tapestry series is the Flemish 'The Lady and the Unicorn', circa 1500, the sixth of which depicts an array of textiles put to different uses. We see clear evidence of an already-multicultural vocabulary of patterns spanning 2,000 miles from Brussels to Damascus. The lady's skirt alone – with its huge pomegranate pattern on a large curving stem – replicates the scale and grace of the patterned velvets for which Venice, Florence and Genoa were then known, and which in turn were indebted to the skills of weavers in Syria, Turkey, Greece and Cyprus. Their warp-pile weaving technique is now thought to have originated in China and travelled westwards along the Silk Roads or with militaristic Mongols. More certain is the production of velvet cloths in Damascus, Syria, at the court of the Umayyad Caliph, Hisham ibn Abd al-Malik (691–743).[7]

Such knowledge is relatively new: for the reference in early Arabic literature to *kutuf* (which may have been the Arabic term for velvet), we are indebted to the scholar and traveller Robert Bertram Serjeant (1915–1993) and his January 1972 book on Islamic textiles.[8] Dr Serjeant's book employed rigorous research methods, taking into account not just the written word, but also real textiles and real people. This present volume employs the same combination, handing forward even more first-hand knowledge.

Although today we might assume that it was within universities that such meticulous studies evolved, that is not the entire story. This book makes that clear too. One cannot really know about objects without seeing them. That is the rationale for museums, which began to form in the mid-19th century. London's Victoria and Albert Museum, founded in 1852 as the Museum of Manufactures, was described by Henry Cole, its first director, as a 'schoolroom for everyone'. As with other museums, such as the Philadelphia Museum of Art (a legacy of the Centennial Exhibition of 1876), its primary mission was to improve the standards of industry by educating designers and acting as an aid to manufacturers.

Philadelphia's textile collection, now totalling well over 15,000 items, was developed primarily through purchases. But, more often than not, museums were, and still are, dependent on the generosity of collectors. Examples include Julius Lessing (1845–1908), the first director of the Berliner Kunstgewerbemuseum, whose curatorial career started in the early 1870s with his presentation of the collection of Crown Prince Frederick and others. One of the first to study paintings as a means of dating carpets, Lessing didn't have sight of many real ones but bequeathed to the world the descriptors for early Turkish carpets with particular distinctive patterns. ('Holbein', for example, refers to carpets such as that depicted in Hans Holbein's *The Ambassadors*, 1533.)

The scarcity of Turkish carpets in Europe did not last long, however, for the age of the department store was dawning. The first of these, Le Bon Marché, had been founded in Paris in 1838; by 1852 it was greeting customers with an 'oriental saloon'. The saloon, especially after expansion in 1869 and 1872, gave full play to 'whole markets of carpets from the Levant' and a 'sumptuous pacha's tent was furnished with divans and armchairs, made with camel sacks, some ornamented with many-coloured lozenges...'.[9] The impact was soon felt in London. There were Oriental Departments in William Whiteley's as well as Debenham and Freebody's, together with the Eastern Baazar opened by Lasenby Liberty in London in 1875. (Today the oldest continuous department is Liberty's Oriental Carpet Room, for which the carpet buyer, Bruce Lepere, handpicks every piece, travelling from the Khyber Pass and the Dasht-e-Kavir desert to the bazaars of Peshawar and the Hindu Kush mountains).

G. P. Baker, whose family had begun in the 1850s as traders of goods via contacts at the British Embassy in Constantinople, was by 1878 importing Persian, Turkish and Turkmen carpets into London, often re-exporting these to Paris and the United States. In 1884 G. P. and J. Baker was formed, ultimately becoming known for its printed and woven textiles, as well as its remarkable archive of some 3,000 Chinese, Turkish, Peruvian, Indian, Indonesian and European textiles (only diminished when 300-plus items were donated to the V&A between ca. 1900 and 1960). In 1907 it joined forces with a consortium

opposite
Panel from the 'Lady and the Unicorn' tapestry series, Flanders, circa 1500. Musée national du Moyen Âge et Thermes de Cluny, Cl. 10833

of Levantine traders, becoming the Oriental Carpet Manufacturers; by 1912 it had offices in London, Paris, Constantinople, Cairo, Alexandria, Sydney, Buenos Aires and New York. The company employed 40,000 weavers in Anatolia alone.[10]

In this way such carpets – and the chenille Axminster imitations provided by James Templeton of Glasgow – became *de rigueur*, and it was increasingly difficult for individuals to find examples first-hand. Yet find them they did. Notable among these collectors was James Franklin Ballard (1851–1931), an entrepreneur made wealthy through his sales of a proprietary medicine that promised a quick and permanent cure for 'all the ills that flesh is heir to'.[11] Having travelled close to half-a-million miles from 1905 in search of objects, Ballard made a 1922 donation to the Metropolitan Museum of Art of 129 carpets. They included Turkish Ushak, Ladik, Bergama, Ghiordes and Kula examples as well as Persian, Caucasian, Central Asian, Indian, Chinese and Spanish rugs. It doubled the museum's carpet collection and at the same time ushered in the acceptance of 'corporate' sponsorship, since Ballard had already displayed a portion of his collection in his private gallery at St Louis, as well as in museums in Minneapolis, Chicago and San Francisco.[12]

With 'elite' carpets now firmly in the hands of specialist dealers, there remained room for smaller dealers in flatwoven kilims and embroideries, used for upholstery and portières. Consumers were encouraged to adopt them by the influential British architect and writer Charles Locke Eastlake (1836–1906), whose *Hints on Household Taste, Upholstery and other Details* enjoyed four editions in the UK (1868 to 1878) and six in the US (1872 to 1881), there spawning a style of furniture named after him. Public appreciation of this art was undoubtedly being expanded by writers such as Eastlake, through department stores, and – in theory – by collectors through their input to museums. However, actually viewing the museum artefacts was typically via short-term displays.

It was during the same period that New York museums, led by the Department of Anthropology staff at the American Museum of Natural History (AMNH), reimagined their outreach to spur on a distinctly American style of textile and dress design. For about a decade from 1915, designers and manufacturers were given unprecedented access to museum ethnographic collections to serve as inspiration, which by 1918 included the Brooklyn Museum's Textile Study Room. Lectures, publications, and a 1919 'Exhibition of Industrial Art in Textiles and Costumes' showcased garments and cloths inspired by museum holdings from Mexico, Central America, Peru, Siberia, the Philippines and Africa, as well as Native American objects. This movement was followed by a wider embrace of material, visual languages and techniques from across the globe inside and outside museums.

Significantly, in relation to the approaches revealed in this volume, Stewart Cullin of Brooklyn was among the first to display ethnological collections as art objects, not as ethnographic specimens. An article by him for *Women's Wear* illustrated African objects under the title 'Inspiration for Modiste Seen in Vogue of Congo Arts'. Acknowledging a French interest in African sculpture since 1905, his 1923 text goes on to say:

Each advance in modern industrial art, whether it be in costumes or decoration, has as its basis some discovery or re-application of elder arts. The new idea in the applied arts always finds its first expression in the fine arts. The interest recently developed in the galleries of New York and Paris in the little known arts of the Congo region must soon affect the dressmaker and interior designer.[13]

Bauhaus-trained artist Anni Albers is the most noted admirer of Peruvian cloths. But she was not the earliest to open her eyes to their influence. Indeed, for Post-Impressionists as well as Modernists, the significance of traditional textiles cannot be overestimated. Nor was their espousal of the cause limited to painted depictions of textiles. The short-lived but very influential Omega Workshops of Post-Impressionist Roger Fry included in their output furnishing fabrics known as 'Manchester batiks'.[14]

Two women designers, Ruth Reeves (1892–1966) and Marion Dorn (1896–1964, known for her Modernist carpets), further helped shift perceptions. In their work

non-Western textiles informed a visual language that adorned the London hotel lobbies of the Savoy and Claridge's (Dorn) while, in New York, Radio City Music Hall since 1932 has retained carpets and wallpapers by Reeves. The latter actively promoted authentic everyday indigenous objects as visual references, in 1935 founding the Index of American Design.[15] Still, far more people visited these rugs than owned anything like them. The shift from admiration to widespread ownership – a key feat achieved by the 1960s and indebted to people such as those interviewed here – required a change in attitudes.

Not surprisingly, that change began as political and geographical boundaries shifted significantly after the First World War. It involved setting aside assumptions and responding to visual media without any preconceived notions. It can be seen in action among young influential interwar designers such as Minnie McLeish, whose exhortation in a 1920 edition of *The Cabinet Maker and Complete House Furnisher* is summed up by her biographer, Keren Protheroe, as:

> ...appealing to consumers to recognise and acknowledge their innate emotional understanding of good colour, rhythm and form – basically, to judge the worth of a textile by whether it feels good in your bones.[16]

Nothing satisfies this ancient and essential form of curiosity more than the stimulation of abstract patterns that tribal arts provide, as the tales captured in this volume amply illustrate.

Among the handful of curators in the 1970s who insisted on global textile art was Mary Hunt Kahlenberg. From 1968–78 she was the head of the costume and textile department at the Los Angeles County Museum of Art (LACMA). Her specialities were Japanese and Indonesian, the latter expressed in the 1977 LACMA exhibition 'Textile Traditions of Indonesia', another landmark show, leading to the post-1978 creation of her own important Indonesian collection. As a private curator for Lloyd E. Cotsen, she built the textile and folk-art collection now housed in his endowed Neutrogena Wing at the Museum of International Folk Art in Santa Fe.

© American Museum of Natural History

But while still at LACMA, Kahlenburg also curated 'Grass', in 1976. The focus on this difficult-to-research topic was chosen because 'objects made of grass provide a valuable if fragile link with centuries of anonymous craftsmen'.[17] Aside from the thrill of seeing the half-canoe protruding from a wall, or the Polish chandelier, there was a Filipino backpack, Japanese raincoat, Mexican mask, Karok Native American skirt and Egyptian necklace. No longer could the Fiber Arts and American Art To Wear movements[18] be said to have had no apparent antecedents, to have seemingly sprung unheeded into life with the young generation of the 1960s. This was a show that provided proof of an ancient and global pedigree, adding further validation to the importance of collecting and understanding non-Western textiles.

———

However much collectors, scholars and designers had gathered items before the Second World War, it had all changed with the combination of independent-minded youth and cheap travel. Films, television and magazines disseminated the hippie lifestyle and its attendant jeans-plus-tribal-whatnot look. There followed decades of excitement for *real* stuff, which transformed what we wore and how we decorated.

The stories within this volume capture both youthful energy and the link to the merchant adventurers and ambassadors of old. Andy Hale is right to say 'There's nothing new about Westerners going to Asia and buying beautiful things. It goes back to Marco Polo.' It may be obvious but seems worth saying: Polo was important because he *wrote things down*, making a contribution as irreplaceable as the contemporary accounts in these pages.

Those interviewed speak of personally finding the need to travel, collect and understand, but so often it transpires that there were travellers, collectors and storytellers in their background. After thousands of years it seems likely that future generations will follow their instincts, too, and they'll now have the advantage of many inspirational books – including this one. They will find other textiles to collect. What we can be sure of is that cloths are not only made to move, but are also designed to move *us* emotionally – and that makes them irresistible.

1   'The thing about archives', in Anna Buruma et al., T*he Liberty Archive Book: The Archivist's Edit*, Liberty, 2021.
2   https://www.worldcat.org/
3   Schoeser, 'Oriental connections: merchant adventurers and the transmission of cultural concepts', in Kathryn Norberg and Sandra Rosenbaum (eds), *Fashion Prints in the Age of Louis XIV*, Texas Tech University Press, 2014.
4   *Le Mercure galant*, founded 1672. Edited by Jean Donneau de Visé, at first sporadically and then from 1677 to 1710 as the monthly gazette *Le Nouveau Mercure galant*. See *Recueil des modes de la cour de France* (bound 1703–04 but images 1678–93) in the public domain at https://collections.lacma.org/node/
5   Craig Sams, the Sweet Jane blog, December 2012; https://sweetjanespopboutique.blogspot.com/2012/05/rise-and-fall-of-afghan-coat-1966-197.html. See also https://theconversation.com/friday-essay-how-afghan-coats-left-kabul-for-the-fashion-world-and-became-a-hippie-must-have-165007
6   https://objectsofartshows.com/partners/
7   https://trc-leiden.nl/trc-digital-exhibition/index.php/velvet/item/173-a-brief-history-of-velvet
8   R. B. Serjeant, *Islamic Textiles: Material for a History up to the Mongol Conquest* (Librairie du Liban, Beirut: 1972). See also https://al-bab.com/albab-orig/albab/bys/obits/serjeant.htm
9   Roger Luckhurst, *The Mummy's Curse: The True History of a Dark Fantasy*, OUP, Oxford, 2012, p. 115, citing Émile Zola, *Au bonheur des dames*, 1883.
10 Jairus Banaji, *A Brief History of Commercial Capitalism*, Haymarket Books, 2020, https://cominsitu.files.wordpress.com/2020/10/jairus-banaji-a-brief-history-of-commercial-capitalism.pdf, p. 63.
11 *The Pioche Weekly Record*, 1906, https://chroniclingamerica.loc.gov/data/batches/nvln_caliente_ver02/data/sn86091348/00415627154/1906030201/0035.pdf [18/12/21]
12 Joseph Breck and Frances Morris, *The James F. Ballard Collection of Oriental Rugs*, The Metropolitan Museum of Art, 1923, https://www.metmuseum.org/art/metpublications/The_James_F_Ballard_Collection_of_Oriental_Rugs
13 Stewart Culin, 'Inspiration for Modiste Seen in Vogue of Congo Arts', *Women's Wear*, 23 March 1923, p. 31.
14 See Schoeser, 'Textiles', in *Beyond Bloomsbury: Designs of the Omega Workshops 1913–1919*, Fontanka for Courtauld Gallery, London, 2009.
15 See Andrew Kelly, *Kentucky by Design: The Decorative Arts, American Culture, and The Index of American Design*, University Press of Kentucky, 2015.
16 Correspondence with the author, 20 December 2021.
17 Mary Hunt Kahlenberg, *Grass*, LACMA, 1976, http://www.lacma.org/sites/default/files/reading_room/images.compressed.pdf
18 See Dilys Blum, Mary Schoeser and Julie Schafler Dale, *Off the Wall: American Art to Wear*, Yale University Press, 2019.

Further reading

Alexander, Christopher Aslan, *A Carpet Ride to Khiva: Seven Years on the Silk Road*. 2010, London, Icon Books

Ames, Frank, *The Kashmir Shawl: And Its Indo-French Influence*. 1999, Woodbridge, Suffolk UK, ACC Art Books

Ames, Frank, *Woven Masterpieces of Sikh Heritage*. 2010, Woodbridge, Suffolk UK, ACC Art Books

Ansary, Tamim, *Games Without Rules: The Often Interrupted History of Afghanistan*. 2012, New York, Public Affairs (Perseus Books)

Askari, Hasan, and Nasreen Askari, *The Flowering Desert: Textiles from Sindh*. 2019, London, Paul Holberton Publishing

Askari, Nasreen, and Liz Arthur, *Uncut Cloth*. 1999, London, Merrell Holberton

Askari, Nasreen, and Rosemary Crill, *Colours of the Indus: Costume and Textiles of Pakistan*. 1997, London, Merrell Holberton in association with the Victoria and Albert Museum

Aslan, Chris, *Unravelling the Silk Road: Travels and Textiles in Central Asia*. 2023, London, Icon Books

Auboyer, Jeannine, *The Art of Afghanistan*. 1968, Middlesex UK, Hamlyn Publishing Group

Baldiserra, Nicolò Castellini, *Inside Tangier: House & Gardens*. 2019, Palm Beach, Vendome Press

Bass, Gary J., *The Blood Telegram: Nixon, Kissinger, and a Forgotten Genocide*. 2013, New York, Alfred A. Knopf

Bennett-Jones, Owen, *Pakistan: Eye of the Storm*. 2009, New Haven and London, Yale University Press

Bennett-Jones, Owen, *The Bhutto Dynasty*. 2020, New Haven and London, Yale University Press

Bergreen, Laurence, *Marco Polo: From Venice to Xanadu*. 2007, New York, Vintage Books

Blum, Dilys, *The Fine Art of Textiles: The Collections of the Philadelphia Museum of Art*. 2006, Philadelphia Museum of Art

Bossert, Helmut Theodore, *Folk Art of Europe*. 1990, New York, Rizzoli

Bouvier, Nicolas, *The Way of the World*. 2009, New York, NYRB Classics, Illustrated edition: Drawings by Thierry Vernet

Byron, Robert, *The Road to Oxiana*. 1937, New York, Oxford University Press

Caryl, Christian, *Strange Rebels: 1979 and the Birth of the 21st Century*. 2013, New York, Basic Books

Chandrasekaran, Rajiv, *Little America: The War within the War for Afghanistan*. 2012, New York, Alfred K. Knopf

Cohen, Roger, *Hearts Grown Brutal: Sagas of Sarajevo*. 2001, New York, Random House

Coll, Steve, *Directorate S: The CIA and America's Secret Wars in Afghanistan and Pakistan*. 2019, London, Penguin Books

Coll, Steve, *Ghost Wars: The Secret History of the CIA, Afghanistan and Bin Laden from the Soviet Invasion to September 10, 2001*. 2004, London, Penguin Books

Coll, Steve, *On the Grand Trunk Road: A Journey into South Asia*. 2009, London, Penguin Books

Cooper, Alanna E., *Bukharan Jews and the Dynamics of Global Judaism*. 2012, Bloomington and Indianapolis, Indiana University Press

Crill, Rosemary, *Indian Ikat Textiles*. 1998, New York, Weatherhill

Crill, Rosemary, *Indian Embroidery*. 1999, London, Victoria and Albert Museum

Crill, Rosemary, *Textiles from India: The Global Trade*. 2006, Kolkata, Seagull Books

Crill, Rosemary, *Chintz: Indian Textiles of the West*. 2008, London, Victoria and Albert Museum

Crill, Rosemary, *V&A Pattern: Indian Florals*. 2009, London, Victoria and Albert Museum

Crill, Rosemary, *The Fabric of India*. 2015, London, Victoria and Albert Museum

Crill, Rosemary et al, *Global Ikat: Roots and Routes of a Textile Technique: The David Paly Collection*. 2023, London, Hali Publications Ltd.

Crites, Mitchell, and Ameeta Nanji, *India Color: Spirit, Tradition and Style*. 2008, San Francisco, Chronicle Books

Dalrymple, William, *The Anarchy: The East India Company, Corporate Violence and the Pillage of an Empire*. 2019, London, Bloomsbury Publishing

De Bellaigue, Christopher, *The Islamic Enlightenment: The Modern Struggle Between Faith and Reason*. 2017, New York, London, Liveright Publishing Corp.

Denny, Walter B., and Sumru Belger Krody, *The Sultan's Garden: The Blossoming of Ottoman Art*. 2012, The Textile Museum, Washington, DC

Denny, Walter B., *How to Read Islamic Carpets*. 2014, New Haven and London, Metropolitan Museum of Art and Yale University Press

Duarte, Ardian, *The Crafts and Textiles of Sind and Balochistan*. 1982, Jamshoro, Pakistan, Institute of Sindhology, University of Sind

Eiland, Murray L., *Oriental Rugs: Expanded Edition.* 1973, 1976, New York Graphic Society

Eiseman, Leatrice, and Keith Recker, *Pantone: The 20th Century in Color.* 2011, San Francisco, Chronicle Books

El Rashidi, Seif, and Sam Bowker, *The Tentmakers of Cairo: Egypt's Medieval and Modern Appliqué Craft.* 2018, New York, The American University in Cairo Press

Elson, Vickie C., *Dowries from Kutch.* 1979, Los Angeles, Museum of Cultural History, University of California

Facing West: Oriental Jews of Central Asia and the Caucasus. 1996, St Petersburg, exhibition catalogue, Russian Museum of Ethnography

Farman-Farma, Nathalie, *Décors Barbares: The Enchanting Interiors of Nathalie Farman-Farma.* 2020, Palm Beach and London, Vendome Press

Fatland, Erika, *Sovietistan.* 2021, New York, Pegasus Books

Fee, Sarah, *Cloth that Changed the World: The Art and Fashion of Indian Chintz.* 2020, London, Yale University Press

Filkins, Dexter, *The Forever War.* 2008, New York, Alfred A. Knopf

Fitz Gibbon, Kate and Andrew Hale, 'The Bad Beys of Central Asia'. 1994, London, in *HALI* 75

Fitz Gibbon, Kate, and Andrew Hale, *Ikat: Splendid Silks of Central Asia: The Goldman Collection.* 1997, London, Laurence King Publishing

Fitz Gibbon, Kate, and Andrew Hale, *Uzbek Embroidery in the Nomadic Tradition.* 2007, Minneapolis Museum of Art

Forbes, Rosita, *Appointment with Destiny.* 1946, New York, E. P. Dutton & Co., Inc.

Forbes, Rosita, ed. Margaret Bald, *From the Sahara to Samarkand: Selected Travel Writings of Rosita Forbes 1919–1937.* 2010, Edinburg, VA, Axios Press

Fotheringham, Avalon, *The Indian Textile Sourcebook.* 2019, London, Thames & Hudson

Frankopan, Peter, *The Silk Roads: A New History of the World.* 2017, New York, Vintage Books

Frater, Judy, *Threads of Identity: Embroidery and Adornment of the Nomadic Rabaris.* 1997, Ahmedabad, Mapin Publishing

Ghosh, Pika, *Making Kantha, Making Home: Women at Work in Colonial Bengal.* 2020, University of Washington Press

Gingeras, Ryan, *The Last Days of the Ottoman Empire 1918–1922.* 2022, London, Allen Lane

Gillow, John, *African Textiles: Colour and Creativity Across a Continent.* 2016, London, Thames & Hudson

Gillow, John, *Printed and Dyed Textiles from Africa.* 2001. London, British Museum Press

Gillow, John, *Textiles of the Islamic World.* 2013, London, Thames & Hudson

Gillow, John, *Traditional Indian Textiles.* 1991, London, Thames & Hudson

Gillow, John, *Traditional Indonesian Textiles.* 1993, London, Thames & Hudson

Gillow, John, and Bryan Sentence, *World Textiles: A Visual Guide to Traditional Techniques.* 2005, London, Thames & Hudson

Gitlin, Todd, *The Sixties: Years of Hope, Days of Rage.* 1987, New York, Bantam Books

Glazebrook, Philip, *Journey to Khiva: A Writer's Search for Central Asia.* 1992, New York, Kodansha America, Inc.

Gomersall, Susan, *Kilim Rugs: Tribal Tales in Wool.* 1999, Atglen, PA, Schiffer Publishing Ltd

Guy, John, and Karun Thakar, *Indian Cotton Textiles: Seven Centuries of Chintz from the Karun Thakar Collection.* 2015, London, Hali Publications Ltd.

Hopkirk, Peter, *Setting the East Ablaze: Lenin's Dream of an Empire in Asia.* 1995, New York, Kodansha International

Hopkirk, Peter, *The Great Game: The Struggle for Empire in Central Asia.* 1994, New York, Kodansha, America, Inc.

Houghteling, Sylvia, *The Art of Cloth in Mughal India.* 2022, Princeton NJ, Princeton University Press

Housego, Jenny, *A Woven Life.* 2020, New Delhi, Roli Books

Howell, Georgina, *Gertrude Bell: Queen of the Desert, Shaper of Nations.* 2006, New York, Farrar, Straus and Giroux

Kalter, Johannes, *The Arts and Crafts of the Swat Valley: Living Traditions in the Hindu Kush.* 1991, London, Thames & Hudson

Kalter, Johannes, *The Arts and Crafts of Turkestan.* 1984, London, Thames & Hudson

Kalter, Johannes, and Margareta Pavaloi, *Uzbekistan: Heirs to the Silk Road.* 1999, London Thames & Hudson

Kaplan, Robert D., *Eastward to Tartary: Travels in the Balkans, the Middle East, and the Caucasus.* 2000, New York, First Vintage Departures Edition, Random House

Kassabova, Kapka, *Border: A Journey to the Edge of Europe.* 2017, London, Graywolf Press

King, Charles, *Midnight at the Pera Palace: The Birth of Modern Istanbul*. 2014, New York, W. W. Norton & Company, Inc.

Krody, Sumru Belger, *Colors of the Oasis: Central Asian Ikats*. 2010, The Textile Museum. Washington, DC

Krody, Sumru Belger, *Flowers of Silk & Gold: Four Centuries of Ottoman Embroidery*. 2000, Merrell, in association with The Textile Museum, Washington, DC

Kwon, Charlotte, and Meena Raste, *Through the Eye of a Needle: Stories from an Indian Desert*. 2003, Vancouver, Maiwa Handprints Ltd

Kwon, Charlotte, and Tim McLaughlin, *Textiles of the Banjara: Cloth and Culture of a Wandering Tribe*. 2016, New York, Thames & Hudson

Langlands, Alastair, *Robert Kime*. 2016, London, Frances Lincoln

Leoni, Francesca, *Aegean Legacies: Greek Island Embroideries from the Ashmolean Museum*. 2021, London, Hali Publications Ltd.

MacLean, Rory, *Magic Bus: On the Hippie Trail from Istanbul to India*. 2006, Brooklyn, New York, Ig Publishing

Maktabi, Hadi, *The Persian Carpet: The Forgotten Years 1722–1872*. 2019, London, Hali Publications Ltd.

Mann, Vivian B. (ed.), *Morocco Jews and Art in a Muslim Land*. 2000, New York, Merrell, in association with The Jewish Museum

Mason, Dariell (ed.), with essays by Cristin McKnight Sethi, *Phulkari: The Embroidered Textiles of Punjab from the Jill and Sheldon Bonovitz Collection*. 2017, Philadelphia Museum of Art

Mehta, Suketu, *Maximum City: Bombay Lost and Found*. 2004, New York, Vintage Books

Meller, Susan, *Russian Textiles: Printed Cloth for the Bazaars of Central Asia*. 2007, New York, Abrams

Meller, Susan, *Silk and Cotton Textiles from the Central Asia that Was*. 2013, New York, Abrams

Morrell, Anne, *Stitches in Gujarati Embroidery*. 2015, Ahmedabad, Sarabhai Foundation

Munayyer, Hanan Karaman, *Traditional Palestinian Costume: Origins and Evolution*. 2020, Northampton MA, Olive Branch Press

Neumann, Helmut & Heidi, *Textiles of India*. 2020, New York and London, Prestel

Opie, James, *Tribal Rugs: A Complete Guide to Nomadic and Village Carpets*. 2016, Vermont, Echo Point Books & Media

Opie, James, *Tribal Rugs of Southern Persia*. 1981, Portland OR, J. Opie Oriental Rugs

Paine, Sheila, *Chikan Embroidery: The Floral Whitework of India*, 1989, London, Shire Publications

Paine, Sheila, *Embroidered Textiles: A World Guide to Traditional Patterns*. 2010, London, Thames & Hudson

Paine, Sheila, *Embroidery from Afghanistan*. 2007, University of Washington

Paine, Sheila, *Embroidery from India and Pakistan*. 2001, University of Washington

Paine, Sheila, *The Afghan Amulet: Travels from the Hindu Kush to Razgrad*. 1994, New York, St Martin's Press

Paine, Sheila, *The Golden Horde: From the Himalaya to the Mediterranean*. 2006, London, Tauris Parke Paperbacks

Paine, Sheila. *The Linen Goddess: Travels from the Red Sea to Prizren*. 2003, London, Pallas Athene

Parsons, R. D., *Oriental Rugs Vol. 3: The Carpets of Afghanistan*. 1983, Woodbridge, Suffolk UK, Antique Collectors Club

Pathak, Anamika, *Pashmina*. 2008, New Delhi, Roli Books

Peck, Amelia, Elena Phipps et al., *Interwoven Globe: The Worldwide Textile Trade 1500–1800*. 2013, New York, Metropolitan Museum of Art

Phillips, Amanda, *Sea Change: Ottoman Textiles between the Mediterranean and the Indian Ocean*. 2021, University of California Press

Postrel, Virginia, *The Fabric of Civilization: How Textiles Made the World*. 2020, New York, Basic Books

Rau, Pip, *Ikats: Woven Silks from Central Asia. The Rau Collection*. 1988, Oxford, Blackwell in cooperation with the Crafts Council

Recker, Keith, *True Colors: World Masters of Natural Dyes and Pigments*. 2020, Loveland, CO, Thrums Books

Recker, Keith, *Deep Color: The Shades that Shape our Souls*. 2022, Atglen, PA, Schiffer

Reed, Stanley, *Oriental Rugs & Carpets*. 1972, London, Octopus

Rehman, Sherry, and Naheed Jafri, *The Kashmiri Shawl: From Jamavar to Paisley*. 2006, Uttar Pradesh, Om Books

Robbins, Kenneth X., and Pushkar Sohoni, *Jewish Heritage of the Deccan: Mumbai, the Northern Konkan and Pune*. 2017, Mumbai, Jaico Publishing House

Rogan, Eugene, *The Fall of the Ottomans: The Great War in the Middle East, 1914–1920*. 2015, London, Allen Lane

Rogerson, Barnaby, and Rose Baring (eds), *Tales from the Life of Bruce Wannell: Adventurer, Linguist, Orientalist*. 2020, London, Sickle Moon Books

Rothberg, Michael, *Nomadic Visions: Tribal Weavings from Persia and the Caucasus*. 2021, London, Hali Publications Ltd.

Sackville-West, Vita, *Twelve Days in Persia: Across the Mountains with the Bakhtiari Tribe*. 2009, London, Tauris Parke Paperbacks

Sassoon, Joseph, *The Sassoons: The Great Global Merchants and Making of an Empire*. 2022, New York, Pantheon

Schoeser, Mary, *Textiles: The Art of Mankind*. 2012, London, Thames & Hudson

Schoeser, Mary, *World Textiles: A Concise History*. 2003, London, Thames & Hudson

Shah, Shilpa, and Rosemary Crill, *The Shoemaker's Stitch: Mochi Embroideries of Gujarat in the TAPI Collection*. 2023, New Delhi, Niyogi Books

Shankar, Ann, and Jenny Housego, *Bridal Durries of India*. 1997, Ahmedabad, Mapin Publishing Pvt. Ltd

Silverman, Eric, *A Cultural History of Jewish Dress*. 2013, London, New York, Bloomsbury Academic

Spurling, Hilary, and Jack Flam, *Matisse: His Art and His Textiles*. 2004, Royal Academy of Arts, London in association with The Metropolitan Museum of Art, New York

Sukhareva, O. A., *Suzani: Central Asian Decorative Embroidery*. 2013, Tashkent, UNESCO, International Institute of Central Asian Studies (IICAS), Samarkand State United Historical-Architectural and Art Museum

Suleman, Fahmida, *Textiles of the Middle East and Central Asia: The Fabric of Life*. 2017, New York, Thames & Hudson

Sumner, Christina, and Guy Petherbridge, *Bright Flowers: Textiles and Ceramics of Central Asia*. 2004, Brooklyn, New York, Powerhouse Publishing

Taylor, Roderick, *Ottoman Embroidery*. 1990, Northampton MA, Interlink Books

Thakar, Karun, Rosemary Crill, Avalon Fotheringham, et al., *Indian Textiles: 1,000 Years of Art and Design*. 2021, London, Hali Publications Ltd.

Tharoor, Shashi, *Inglorious Empire: What the British Did to India*. 2016, UK, Scribe Publications

Theroux, Paul, *The Great Railway Bazaar: By Train Through Asia*. 1975, Boston, New York, Houghton Mifflin Company

Tsareva, Elena, *Turkmen Carpets: Masterpieces of Steppe Art, from 16th to 19th Centuries: The Hoffmeister Collection*. 2011, Stuttgart, Arnoldsche Art Publishers

Tsareva, Elena, *Turkmen Carpets: The Neville Kingston Collection*. 2016, Stuttgart, Arnoldsche Art Publishers

Tschebull, Raoul E., *Qarajeh to Quba: Rugs and Flatweaves from East Azarbayjan and the Transcaucasus*. 2019, London, Hali Publications Ltd.

Vogelsang-Eastwood, Gillian, *Dressed with Distinction: Garments from Ottoman Syria*. 2020, Los Angeles, Fowler Museum at UCLA

Vogelsang-Eastwood, Gillian, *Encylopedia of Embroidery from Central Asia, the Iranian Plateau and the Indian Subcontinent*. 2021, London, Bloomsbury Visual Arts

Walsh, Declan, *The Nine Lives of Pakistan: Dispatches from a Precarious State*. 2021, London, Bloomsbury Publishing

Weir, Shelagh, *Embroidery from Palestine*. 2007, University of Washington Press

Weir, Shelagh, and Serene Shahid, *Palestinian Embroidery*. 1988, London, British Museum Press

Whitfield, Susan, *Life along the Silk Road*. 1999, University of California Press

Zaman, Niaz, *The Art of Kantha Embroidery*. 2014, Dhaka, University Press Ltd, Bangladesh